THE EVERYTHING EASY LARGE-PRINT WORD SEARCH BOOK

VOLUME 7

Dear Reader,

I think that sometimes simpler is better. That's why I love word search puzzles. You don't need to login, download, swipe the screen, or call tech support. The only power required here is from your brain as it gets a healthy workout. Word search puzzles are a refreshing change in today's hi-tech world.

I had a blast creating this book for you. Each puzzle has a theme and there is a wide range of topics. Loads of relevant words have been hidden in each grid. It will take you a while to complete each puzzle. But with enough dedication, all of the words can be found—there are no stumpers here! To make the solving more pleasant, we've used large print that is easy on the eyes.

So grab this book whenever you want some brain-boosting fun. All that's needed is a pencil (or pen) and a bit of free time. Happy searching!

Charles Timmerman

Welcome to the EVERYTHING Series!

These handy, accessible books give you all you need to tackle a difficult project, gain a new hobby, comprehend a fascinating topic, prepare for an exam, or even brush up on something you learned back in school but have since forgotten.

You can choose to read an Everything® book from cover to cover or just pick out the information you want from our four useful boxes: e-questions, e-facts, e-alerts, and e-ssentials. We give you everything you need to know on the subject, but throw in a lot of fun stuff along the way, too.

We now have more than 400 Everything® books in print, spanning such wide-ranging categories as weddings, pregnancy, cooking, music instruction, foreign language, crafts, pets, New Age, and so much more. When you're done reading them all, you can finally say you know Everything®!

PUBLISHER Karen Cooper

MANAGING EDITOR, EVERYTHING® SERIES Lisa Laing

COPY CHIEF Casey Ebert

ASSISTANT PRODUCTION EDITOR Jo-Anne Duhamel

ACQUISITIONS EDITOR Lisa Laing

EVERYTHING® SERIES COVER DESIGNER Erin Alexander

Visit the entire Everything® series at *www.everything.com*

THE EVERYTHING® EASY LARGE-PRINT WORD SEARCH BOOK

VOLUME 7

More than 100 new easy-to-read puzzles

Charles Timmerman
Founder of Funster.com

Adams Media
New York London Toronto Sydney New Delhi

Adams Media
An Imprint of Simon & Schuster, Inc.
100 Technology Center Drive
Stoughton, MA 02072

An Everything® Series Book.
Everything® and everything.com® are registered trademarks of Simon & Schuster, Inc.

For information about special discounts for bulk purchases, please contact Simon & Schuster Special Sales at 1-866-506-1949 or business@simonandschuster.com.

The Simon & Schuster Speakers Bureau can bring authors to your live event. For more information or to book an event contact the Simon & Schuster Speakers Bureau at 1-866-248-3049 or visit our website at www.simonspeakers.com.

Manufactured in the United States of America

7 2023

Library of Congress Cataloging-in-Publication Data has been applied for.

ISBN 978-1-4405-9780-0

Dedicated to my brother Steve

Acknowledgments

I would like to thank each and every one of the more than half a million people who have visited my website, Funster.com, to play word games and puzzles. You have shown me how much fun puzzles can be and how addictive they can become!

It is a pleasure to acknowledge the folks at Adams Media who made this book possible. I particularly want to thank my editor, Lisa Laing, for so skillfully managing the many projects we have worked on together.

Contents

Contents

Introduction

The puzzles in this book are in the traditional word search format. Words in the list are hidden in the puzzle in any direction: up, down, forward, backward, or diagonal. The words are always found in a straight line, and letters are never skipped. Words can overlap. For example, the two letters at the end of the word "MAST" could be used as the start of the word "STERN." Only uppercase letters are used, and any spaces in an entry are removed. For example, "TROPICAL FISH" would be found in the puzzle as "TROPICALFISH." Apostrophes and hyphens are also omitted in the puzzles. Draw a circle around each word you find. Then cross the word off the list so you will always know which words remain to be found.

A favorite strategy is to look for the first letter in a word, then see if the second letter is one of the neighboring letters, and so on until the word is found. Or instead of searching for the first letter in a word, it is sometimes easier to look for letters that stand out, like Q, U, X, and Z. Double letters in a word will also stand out and be easier to find. Another strategy is to simply scan each row, column, and diagonal looking for any words.

Puzzles

ABSURD

AMUSING

ANECDOTE

CARD

CHUCKLE

CLEVER

CLOWN

COMIC

DROLL

FACE

FUNNY

GAG

GIGGLE

GREETING

HOAX

IMPROV

JEST

JOKE

LAMPOON

LAUGH

LINE

MISTAKES

MOVIE

PLAY

PRANK

QUOTE

SATIRE

SAYING

SHOW

SILLY

SKETCH

SKIT

SMILE

SONG

SPOOF

STICKER

STORY

VIDEO

WITTY

WRY

Funny Stuff

```
P O V V S T O R Y E T O U Q
S F G I G G L E I S K G S T
U C A R D L X V Y O M K K G
X M D C M E O E H C I Y N W
G C N N E M O L O T S I A W
X N E X A N E C D O T E R I
A S O C H U C K L E A D P T
O B G S T I C K E R K U A T
H G U A L K L R A I E B F Y
S K E T C H G A M U S I N G
G Z S I D A S P M U Y N W J
Q E M R G M R I R P U A O R
J O O E I O S D L F O K L W
C L N L V Y H L L L E O C P
L I E I F O O P S A Y I N G
L V Y I H N W R Y V R G Y X
```

Solution on Page 258

AROMATIC	ODOR
BATH	OILS
CHAMOMILE	OLFACTORY
CLOVE	PERFUME
CURATIVE	PLANTS
DIFFUSED	PLEASANT
DROPLETS	ROSES
ESSENCE	SCENTS
ETHEREAL	SENSORY
FLORAL	SMELL
FRAGRANCE	SPIRITUAL
GAS	STEAM
HEALTH	ULTRASONIC
INCENSE	VAPORIZER
INFUSION	VOLATILE
INHALED	
LAVENDER	
MASSAGE	
MEDICINE	
MIST	
MUSK	
NEBULIZER	

```
S Q R P I N F U S I O N L C
C P L A N T S T E L P O R D
E I S C E N T S F J E C E S
N E T H E R E A L V L L D E
I C O A V S C B I W A O I S
C T I D M T N T U H U V F O
I N L N O O A E N L T E F R
D A S R O R R I C S I K U E
E S Y U U S G A I N R Z S Z
M A T C C H A M O M I L E I
H E A L T H R R A G P L D R
T L A R O L F I T E S E Y O
A P R E D N E V A L T M F P
B M A S S A G E Q M U S K A
E S S E N C E L I T A L O V
E M U F R E P Y R O S N E S
```

Solution on Page 258

BAT

CATCH

CHEER

COACH

COTTON CANDY

DIAMOND

DIRT

DUGOUT

FANS

FRANKS

GAME

GLOVES

GRANDSTAND

HELMET

HOME RUN

INFIELD

INNING

MOUND

MUSIC

ORGAN

PARKING

PEANUTS

PLATE

POINTS

POPCORN

PRETZELS

REFRESHMENTS

SAFE

SCORE

SEATS

SNACKS

SOCCER

SODA

SPECTATORS

STADIUM

STRIKE

TEAM

TICKETS

UMPIRE

UNIFORM

```
X G Y D N A C N O T T O C S
S L C G G D N U O M U S I C
P O S K N A R F O S E P D O
R V D N I I F E P K E N C R
E E F A N S K L I A O A R E
T S F G N B A R N M T S T I
Z T F R I T T U A C U P S S
E A I O E S T I H P O E O A
L D N A T S D N A R G C C F
S I F U N I H H C P U T C E
N U I N R T C M H O D A E U
A M E I O E E K E I I T R T
C P L F C M M H E N R O A O
K I D O P L A O R T T R J B
S R F R O E G F H S S S J F
T E A M P H C A O C S Z O A
```

Solution on Page 258

AMERICA

ANGLICANS

BRADFORD

BROWNIST

CAPE COD

CARGO

CITIZENS

COLONY

DEBT

ENGLISH

EXPLORER

FLEEING

GROWTH

HISTORY

JOHN SMITH

LANDING

LAWS

LEGACY

MASSASOIT

MAYFLOWER

NEW WORLD

PATUXET

PERMANENT

PILGRIMS

PLYMOUTH

RELIGIOUS

RIGHTS

ROCK

SAIL

SETTLERS

SPEEDWELL

SQUANTO

SUCCESS

SURVIVAL

WAR

WINTER

```
R O C K B R A D F O R D H T
T B E D E X P L O R E R T E
S Q U A N T O R E T N I W X
I N C A P E C O D K K G O U
N M A Y F L O W E R Y H R T
W L C C Y L A W S T V T G A
O A I A I Q D E E I J S C P
R V R G R L T N S O F P I L
B I E E E T G M H S L E T Y
S V M L L L I N A A A E E I M
U R A E I R S I A S E D Z O
C U R S G M L D R S I W E U
C S H L I P E R M A N E N T
E S I T O G R A C M G L S H
S P H Z U G N I D N A L C T
S R H I S T O R Y N O L O C
```

Solution on Page 258

ALT

ARROW

BUTTONS

CAPS LOCK

CLICK

COMMANDS

COMMUNICATION

COMPUTER

CONTROL

CTRL

DELETE

ENTER

ESC

FAST

FINGERS

FUNCTION

INPUT

INSERT

INTERNET

KEYS

LAPTOP

LETTERS

MONITOR

MOUSE

NUMBERS

PAGE UP

PUNCTUATION

QWERTY

RETURN

SHIFT

SHORTCUTS

SIGNS

SPACE

SYMBOLS

TAB

TOUCH

TYPE

WORDS

WRITE

```
W R I T E I S L E T T E R S
G M D G Q Y L A P T O P P R
N U M B E R S N G I S U L E
O O I K A R B R E T N E O G
I A I C O M M A N D S G R N
T R E T U R N A T H H H A T I
A R S C A P S L O C K P N F
C O L D R U A R U B F T O U
I W O E E S T O T U E M C L
N O B L T C T C N R M O U R
U R M E U Y P C N O E U F T
M D Y T P R T E N U A S I C
M S S E M I T I O F P E N L
O Y S N O T T U B A A O P I
C C N N C O G D C L Q S U C
D Q W E R T Y E S H I F T K
```

Solution on Page 259

AEROBIC	MUSIC
BENCH	PARTNER
BICEPS	PECS
BICYCLE	PILATES
BOTTLE	POOL
BURN	QUADS
CALVES	REP
CARDIO	ROPES
CLASS	RUNNING
CRUNCHES	SET
CURL	SHOES
DIPS	SPOT
FITNESS	STEPPER
GLOVES	TRACK
GLUTES	TRICEPS
GRIPS	WATER
JOG	WEIGHTS
LAPS	YOGA
LIFT	
LOCKER	
MATS	
MEN	

Fitness Club

```
B I C E P S T E P P E R S N
K S T H G I E W G N E C V M
U T S T R T Q H S L E Q U S
W A P E R X M S C P O S M E
N M T Y V A A Y I N I V S O
I A P O O L C L B C U R E H
W G J J C I A K O B S R G S
I O Y U B T B C R S O P C H
G Y R M E N O R E N T R A P
Z L X S F G T N A C B U T L
P S X D L N T R I C E P S F
R P D A I I L A P A N R U B
Q O I U F N E C N R C X E P
G T P Q T N L W O D H P Q N
V Z S E T U L G V I W T E S
Y Z X Y S R D O L O C K E R
```

Solution on Page 259

PUZZLES • 23

APPOINTMENT

BANK

BILL

BUSY

CHECKLIST

CHIROPRACTOR

CLEANERS

DANCE CLASS

DAY PLANNER

DOCTOR

DRIVE

ENDLESS

EXHAUSTING

GASOLINE

GIFT WRAPPING

GROCERY

HARDWARE

LIBRARY

MAIL

MEETING

NEEDS

OVERWHELMED

POST OFFICE

RETURN MOVIES

SCHEDULES

SCHOOL

SOCCER MOMS

TASKS

TREAT

VOLUNTEER WORK

```
G N I T S U A H X E Y R T C
M N B S D E E N G K R R P L
E N I L O S A G I N E I K E
E N R T L C Z C F A C R C A
L N B O E I C J T B O E H N
D E D N T E B E W W R T E E
E C D L N C M R R V G U C R
M I A I E J A E A M C R K S
L F N A M S E R P R O N L E
E F C M T T S A P D Y M I L
H O E B N A C W I O D O S U
W T C U I S H D N C R V T D
R S L S O K O R G T I I Z E
E O A Y P S O A Q O V E H H
V P S R P E L H D R E S T C
O U S D A Y P L A N N E R S
```

Solution on Page 259

AMAZING

BEAUTIFUL

BOSS

BREATHTAKING

BRILLIANT

DANDY

DYNAMITE

EXCELLENT

FABULOUS

FANTASTIC

FINE

GOOD

GREAT

GROOVY

IMPRESSIVE

INCREDIBLE

MARVELOUS

NEAT

NIFTY

RAD

REGAL

REMARKABLE

SPECTACULAR

SPLENDID

STUNNING

STUPENDOUS

SUPER

SURPRISING

SWEET

TREMENDOUS

UNBELIEVABLE

UNFATHOMABLE

WONDERFUL

```
S U O L E V R A M A Z I N G
L U F R E D N O W N I F T Y
U M F A B U L O U S N E A T
G N I S I R P R U S U P E R
E L B A M O H T A F N U R S
L B R E A T H T A K I N G U
B E E E L D Y N A M I T E O
R A M G L I D R F I N E V D
I U A R N B E I E S R X I N
L T R O G I I V D G W C S E
L I K O R O N D A N A E S P
I F A V A Z O N E B E L E U
A U B Y D N A D U R L L R T
N L L R A L U C A T C E P S
T R E M E N D O U S S N M S
B O S S C F A N T A S T I C
```

Solution on Page 259

ALLEY

ART

BLOCKS

BUS

CITY

CLUBS

COMMUTE

CONCRETE

CORE

CROWD

CULTURE

DENSE

DINING

DIVERSITY

ELEVATOR

ENERGIZED

FAST

HUB

LIGHTS

LINES

LIVELY

LOUD

MUSEUM

NEIGHBORS

NOISE

OFFICES

OPERA

ORDINANCE

POLICE

PUBLIC

SHOPPING

SIRENS

SPRAWL

STADIUM

STATION

STORE

STREETS

SUBWAY

TAXI

THEATER

```
D E N S E R O C A Y T C S X
Z W G U D Q C L R H U B T K
A K O Y T I S R E V I D E R
L S M R T K C A P S Z E E A
L I T Y C C T O O U S Z R C
X S N O R E I T N B J I T O
L U L E R U T L U C E G S M
R B I C S E E L B L R R F M
X W V I T G C U E U O E S U
M A E L A V N V D B P N T T
U Y L O T L A I H U E E A E
S I Y P I T N G P R O L D S
E X W G O I I T I P L L I I
U A H R N E D S Q E O K U O
M T Q G N T R A Y S M H M N
S P R A W L O F F I C E S H
```

Solution on Page 260

ACTION
BEDROCK
BLASTING
CLIFF
COASTAL
COLLUVIUM
DEBRIS
DETACHED
EROSION
FAILURE
FALLING
FORCE
FRAGILE
GLACIERS
GRAVITY
GROUND
LANDSLIP
LOADS
LOGGING
MELTING
MOVEMENTS
OFFSHORE

PRONE
RAINS
REGOLITH
ROCKFALL
SHAPE
SLOPE
SLUMP
SNOW
SOIL
STRUCTURE
TOPPLING
TSUNAMIS
WEAKENING
WILDFIRE

```
G R A V I T Y O P G F S I V
E L I G A R F L N Q L P R N
I E C R O F A I L U R E W O
R A I N S T N E M E V O M I
E P A H S E A P R H N U S S
I V O A K C X U G S I D I O
K R O A T P T N I V E F M R
E C E I V C I R U T S F A E
R W O S U T B L A S T I N G
I N O R L E L C S O I L U O
F Y T E D O H O D D O C S L
D S M I C E P E G N N B T I
L D D C D K B E N G U A Q T
I A F A L L I N G O I O L H
W O E L L A F K C O R N R K
E L C G N I L P P O T P G G
```

Solution on Page 260

ADHESIVES	MEMO BOOK
BOXES	NOTEBOOKS
BUBBLE WRAP	ORGANIZER
CALENDAR	PAPER
CAMERA	PASTE
CHAIR	PENS
CLIPS	PLANNER
COMPUTER	RIBBONS
COPIER	RULER
DESK	SCANNER
EASEL	SCISSORS
ELASTICS	STAMPS
EQUIPMENT	STICKY NOTES
ERASER	TABS
FASTENERS	TACKS
FOLDERS	TAPE
FORMS	TONER
GLUE	TYPEWRITER
INK	
LABELS	
LIGHTS	
MARKER	

```
S P I L C K R R R R T A B S R
T E N Q A R O U I E U S K E
A N K H L E A O L B N K C N
M S R S E T D N B E B O A N
P D E C N I H L X O R O T A
S O N I D R E K R A M B N C
C R N T A W S C O P I E R S
I G A S R E I H T A L T M L
S A L A E P V A N P I O W E
S N P L M Y E I E E G N F B
O I A E A T S R M R H L O A
R Z S G C C O M P U T E R L
S E T O N Y K C I T S S M T
S R E D L O F E U L G A S A
E R A S E R G N Q K S E D P
B O X E S R E N E T S A F E
```

Solution on Page 260

ACCIDENT

BLINKERS

BLOCK

BUMPERS

CAR

CHOKE

CITY

CLOG

CROWD

DETOUR

DRIVING

EXIT

FREEWAY

GRIDLOCK

HIGHWAY

HINDER

HONKING

HORNS

INTERSECTION

INTERSTATE

LANE

LIGHTS

MOVING

OBSTACLE

PATIENCE

RAMP

ROADS

ROUTE

SLOW

SNARL

STILL

STOP

STREET

TIME

TRAVEL

TRUCK

VEHICLES

WAIT

WRECK

YIELD

Slow Traffic

```
P T R U C K N U G C D U B D
E H X H G C O N P W K U R R
K Z O O G N I V O M M O O L
C K L R S K T R D P A M U R
E C C E N R C H E D V R T A
R R W O V S E R S R E A E N
W K H E L A S K T I H C H S
K P C R T B R N N V I M Y T
Z F A O E A E T H I C Q I L
X R Y T L D T L F N L X E L
N E T L I D N S C G E B L A
Y E I C I E I I R A S I D N
W W C R H G N R H E T T Y E
Y A W H G I H C G S T S O Y
L Y I Y R U O T E D B N B P
E M I T E E R T S L O W I O
```

Solution on Page 260

PUZZLES • 35

AQUARIUM

ATTENTION

BATHE

BED

BOWLS

BREED

CAGE

COLLAR

CRATE

CUDDLE

DIET

EXERCISE

FEED

FENCE

GROOM

HANDLING

HAPPINESS

HEALTH

HOME

HOUSING

HYGIENE

KENNEL

LEASH

LITTER

MEDICINE

NAILS

NEUTER

NUTRITION

REGISTER

RUN

SAFETY

SHAMPOO

SUPPLIES

TOYS

TRAIN

TREATS

VET

WALK

WATER

YARD

```
B R E E D R A L L O C N W U
B F N S C N Q T X E I A U T
C B E D I R U A R A T O Y S
I D I E O C A T R E Z R H L
Q U G P D H R T R U A A I W
M B Y D O O I E E I N T H O
O A H M S U U N X D T A S B
O T E C U S M T L E P I E K
R H A Y P I L I R P C G O J
G E L D P N N O I A A N R N
C K T O L G E N I C I D E M
V U H U I R E T S I G E R F
E N D S E S H A M P O O N D
T E I D S N A I L S T W R I
H S A E L E N N E K L A W A
I K S A F E T Y W G Y O B J
```

Solution on Page 261

ACEH
ANGKLUNG
ASEAN
ASIA
BALI
BANTEN
BORNEO
COUNTRY
DENPASAR
DISTRICTS
DIVERSITY
INDOMIE
ISLAM
JAKARTA
JAVA
KALIMANTAN
KELIMUTU
KOMODO
KUPANG
MAJAPAHIT
MANADO
MANOKWARI

OCEANIA
PALU
PAPUA
PONTIANAK
POPULATION
PROVINCES
REBELLION
REPUBLIC
SRIVIJAYA
SUHARTO
TOURISM
TRADE
WILDERNESS
YOGYAKARTA

```
C I L B U P E R M D A I S A
O E N R O B A A I N A E C O
U L A P A S N S U H A R T O
N D Q L A O T O U R I S M G
T I I P K R E B E L L I O N
R V N W I L D E R N E S S Y
Y E A C N O I T A L U P O P
D R T S S N E T N A B G L S
I S R E E J N P M H Y E R U
O I A C M A J A P A H I T T
D T D N M K N N K E V M K U
O Y E I J A V A C I P O U M
M A L V D R R A J T J D P I
O A P O N T I A N A K N A L
K Z F R A A Y M A L S I N E
A P A P U A N G K L U N G K
```

Solution on Page 261

APPLE

BONFIRE

BROWN

CATS

CHILLY

CIDER

COBWEB

COOL

CORN

COSTUMES

FALL

FESTIVAL

FOLIAGE

FOOTBALL

GHOSTS

GOURD

HALLOWEEN

HARVEST

HAYRIDE

HIKING

HOMECOMING

HUES

LEAVES

MAPLE

NOVEMBER

OCTOBER

OFFERING

ORANGE

PLENTY

PUMPKIN

RAIN

RAKE

SCARECROW

SCHOOL

SEASON

SEPTEMBER

SPIDER

SWEATER

TREES

TURKEY

```
T U R K E Y S C H O O L Z R
G S E V A E L H A Y R I D E
O P T R S E A S O N A M C B
U I A A B R O W N P N Q O O
R D E K V S S E U H G R R T
D E W E H A L L O W E E N C
R R S E P T E M B E R B F O
E T W O R C E R A C S M E P
D B L E F C O S T U M E S U
I Z E O O F U O F Z L V T M
C S G M O S E O B P J O I P
G H I N T C L R P E F N V K
C N I S B I E A I T W A A I
G A O L A E R I F N O B L N
R H T G L H I K I N G V O L
G W E S L Y T N E L P A M C
```

Solution on Page 261

ART

BEDDING

BICYCLE

BLANKETS

CANDLES

CHAIR

CHEAP

CLOTHES

COSTUME

DRAPERY

DRESS

FRAYED

FURNITURE

KEEPSAKE

LAMPS

MIRROR

OLD

OUTDATED

PANTS

PHONE

PILLOWS

PLANTER

POSTER

PURSE

RADIO

RETRO

SHABBY

SHIRT

SHOES

TATTERED

TIE

TOYS

TREASURE

TRICYCLE

TRINKETS

UMBRELLA

USED

UTENSILS

VINTAGE

WORN

```
Y B B A H S S S P M A L W U
R E L C Y C I R T O I D A R
E K A S P E E K I N S B D R
T N N B T I L S F A A T R E
N R K U E E L C E R H P E T
A O E C S R K L Y H A C S R
L W T R O L U N O C T Y S O
P R S Y U S I S I W I O E O
A O H R T T T S A R S B L D
E R I E D U I U N E T D D C
H R R P A L S N M E R R N N
C I T A T M D E R E T T A T
U M B R E L L A D U S U C O
E B E D D I N G T A F R N Y
P H O N E G A T N I V N U S
S X S E O H S T J S E Z M P
```

Solution on Page 261

APPLE

AROMA

BAKE

BOX

BROWNIES

CAKE

CHERRY

CHOCOLATE

COFFEE

COOKIES

CREAM

CRULLER

CUSTARD

DANISH

DOUGH

DOZEN

FILLING

FLAVORS

FRY

GLAZE

GREASE

HOLE

HONEY

ICED

ICING

JELLY

MAPLE

NAPKINS

OVEN

PASTRY

PLAIN

RASPBERRY

RING

ROLL

ROUND

STRAWBERRY

STRUDEL

SUGAR

TWIST

VANILLA

Yummy Donuts

```
G H N E Z O D O U G H T P T
K N F F J A L L I N A V Y W
A L I G K E H G N I C I D I
E P D R A T S U C L D A A S
R E P L A I N H V L N E Y T
S Z F L B R O W N I E S C Q
T A G F E C K I S F P H C I
R L R A O D Z H C R E A M B
A G E L I C U S A R O M A O
W R A S P B E R R Y S K P X
B T S L J I P Y T R E B L E
E Q E E K A C H O S A N E L
R T L O S N E V O L Y G O O
R L O T Q N A P K I N S U H
Y C R U L L E R O U N D G S
A Y G A F R Y R J L L O R X
```

Solution on Page 262

ADVERTISING

ALE

AMBER

ANHEUSER

BAR

BEVERAGE

BOTTLE

BRANDS

BREW

BUD

CAN

COLD

CONSUMPTION

COORS

CRAFT

DARK

DRAFT

DRINK

FLAVOR

FOAM

GRAIN

HEAD

HOPS

INDUSTRY

KEG

LAGER

LIGHT

MILLER

MUG

PABST

PARTY

PILSNER

PINT

PROHIBITION

PUB

SCHLITZ

STEAM BEER

STOUT

TAP

YEAST

Solution on Page

```
P L A I J R H M T Y F K W Q
A D B K R A D L O C T P Z M
B S R O O C U I K N I R D K
S E O A T X B G I N E G A Q
T D V I F T Z H T S R N D P
U Y A E A T L T U A O M V Q
O R L L R V P E I I I P E B
T E F A C A H N T L C Z R P
S N B G T N G I L A H E T F
A S T E A M B E E R W C I P
E L R R Z I R B R A N D S J
Y I N Q H Y R T S U D N I X
M P C O N S U M P T I O N F
Q A R E B M A D A E H J G Z
N P N U B L U O H O P S E L
H E P L E M L G V N F X K K
```

Solution on Page 262

ACROBAT

ACTS

AMERICAN

ANIMALS

AUDIENCE

BIG TOP

BROTHERS

CARNIVAL

CHILDREN

CIRCUS

CLOWN

COMPANY

COSTUMES

COTTON CANDY

DOGS

ELEPHANT

ENTERTAINMENT

FAMILY

FUN

GORILLA

GREATEST

HORSES

JUMBO

LAUGH

LION

MAGIC

MONKEYS

MUSIC

PEANUTS

PERFORMERS

POPCORN

RIDES

RING

STADIUM

TENT

TICKETS

TIGER

TRAIN

TRICKS

Solution on page 202.

```
F A M I L Y F U N I A R T P
P C L O W N C H I L D R E N
E L E P H A N T L U T R N R
A M R Z R P M I D A F I T O
N O M Y I M R E B O O D E C
U N A D N O Y O R M G E R P
T K G N G C R M V I D S T O
S E I A B C E B D A C L A P
T Y C C A R N I V A L A I M
A S O N S E O G C Q G M N U
D T S O E G N T S B S I M S
I E T T S I H O H K U N E I
U K U T R T D P I E C A N C
M C M O O B M U J L R I T T
Q I E C H H G U A L I S R Q
M T S E T A E R G A C T S T
```

Solution on Page 262

AFFECTIONATE

ANCESTRY

ANIMAL

BRUSH

CALICO

CAT FLAP

CATNIP

CHASE

CLAWS

CLIMB

COLLAR

CUDDLE

DANDER

FELINE

FUN

HISS

KITTEN

KNEADING

LAZY

LITTER

LOVED

MEOW

MILK

MOUSE

PAW

PET

PUFF

PURR

SCRATCH

SIAMESE

SLEEP

SOFT

STROKE

TABBY

TAIL

TOY

TREE

TRILL

WEAN

YARN

```
A V E R F S A B P A W E A N
P F R B O X S S E S U O M E
P U F F M L W W G L O V E D
P L T E E I D A N A D R J M
C I F E C A L L I M T D F S
A T P I N T A C D I O D U E
M T E D E Z I F A N Y K N C
I E E P T B E O E A S S I H
L R D B T N R T N E H I C R
K L O C I L A C K A C A A U
H O I L K B E O K O T M R X
Y S E R B S R S L F A E X W
L F U Y T T L L L X R S M N
A K X R S Q A A I J C E R N
V P Y E B R P V Z E S A H C
K F W J V J C L G Y Y M I F
```

Solution on Page 262

ALAMOGORDO	RED BLUFF
APACHE	RED RIVER
AZTEC	ROSWELL
BERNALILLO	SANTA FE
CARLSBAD	SCARLET
CARRIZOZO	SOCORRO
CLAYTON	SOUTHWEST
CLOVIS	STATE
CREOSOTE	TAOS
CULTURE	TERRITORY
DEMING	TOM UDALL
GALLUP	TUCUMCARI
GOLD	
LAS CRUCES	
LORDSBURG	
LOS ALAMOS	
LOS LUNAS	
LOVINGTON	
MORA	
MOSQUERO	
MOUNTAINS	
PUEBLO	

```
S E T O S O E R C E T Z A R
K T H O Y R O T I R R E T E
I R A C M U C U T T A O S D
R L O T A U F F U L B D E R
M N A S E P D D C O A P W I
S O O S W B A A U S W U H V
N T R T C E R R L A G E T E
I Y R A G R L X T L R B U R
A A O P I N U L U A U L O S
T L C Z U A I C R M B O S A
N C O G O L D V E O S S I N
U Z S X C I L Z O S D L V T
O D A B S L R A C L R U O A
M S C A R L E T G A O N L F
X Q O D R O G O M A L A C E
G N I M E D O R E U Q S O M
```

Solution on Page 263

BANTER

BIKE

BOWL

CIRCUS

COMEDY

CONCERT

DANCE

DATE

ENJOY

EXCITEMENT

FISH

FRIENDS

GAMES

GOLF

HIKE

JOKES

JUMP

KARAOKE

MOVIES

MUSEUM

PAINTING

PARK

PICNIC

PLAY

POOL

READ

RELAX

RIDE

RUN

SHOPPING

SING

SKI

SLEDDING

SPA

SWIM

TOYS

TRAVEL

TRIP

VISIT

ZOO

```
X N S S P A J S E I D J V W
T V J I B O W L L E C N A D
A D R D K L O E T P O P Q D
S T A E S K V L M L N I F Q
N Y S E M A G U U A C C T G
T I O I R R J R S Y E N N N
Y K W T B A N T E R R I E I
S S E I V O M N U R T C M S
Q U P A R K U G M N H O E C
H S C S L E D D I N G S T C
U F D R F T C A Z E E K I H
N O G N I P P O H S L E C F
P B Z S E C O H M E Q N X A
C C I D K I X A L E R J E C
P V I Q I H R E T A D O W A
P R S O B I J F L O G Y M R
```

Solution on Page 263

BLINDING

BOOTS

CLIMATE

CLOUDS

DARK

DELUGE

DOWNPOUR

DREARY

DRENCHED

DRIZZLE

DROPS

FLOOD

GENTLE

GUTTER

HAIL

HARSH

HEAVY

HURRICANE

INTENSE

MONSOON

MUD

PONCHO

POURING

PUDDLE

RAIN

SHELTER

SLICK

SOAK

SOOTHING

SPRING

STORM

SUMMER

TEMPEST

THUNDER

TORNADO

UMBRELLA

VIOLENT

WATER

WET

WIND

```
G W A T E R S G N I R P S H
I Z J G E T E M P E S T E I
S T O O B R E T T U G A D T
D N I W T N E L O I V R D O
U P U D D L E D K Y E X U R
O F G L Z H S K N A E L M N
L M N Z S G N I R U O P B A
C L I M A T E Y B A H S R D
A R D G E N T L E D D T E O
D E N W M O N S O O N H L O
S M I H N P I P U W C S L L
L M L S O O T H I N G R A F
I U B N I A R K E P H A I L
C S C U S T O R M O Y H F K
K H S P O R D E G U L E D S
O T O S E N A C I R R U H G
```

Solution on Page 263

BINGO

BOARD

BOGGLE

BONDING

CARDS

CHANCE

CHARADES

CHESS

CHIPS

CLUE

COMPETE

DEAL

DICE

DOMINOES

DRINKS

FAMILY

FRIENDS

GO FISH

LAUGHTER

LIFE

LOSER

MONOPOLY

PIECES

POKER

PUZZLES

RISK

RULES

SCRABBLE

SHUFFLE

SNACKS

SORRY

SPADES

SPINNER

TABOO

TEAMS

TOKENS

TROUBLE

TURN

WIN

YAHTZEE

```
T B S P I H C B O A R D X F
E V R E K O P T O K E N S N
A S O R D E E C B G I J V R
M E S S U A T H A W G V W U
S C L S D L P E D E A L E T
K E M A B N E S P I N N E R
N I O X U I E S E M G N Z O
I P N N N G N I D N O B T U
R G O F I S H G R L S C H B
D K P A P M P T O F C I A L
A S O M S B O S E H R B Y E
Y I L I K S E D A R A H C C
E R Y L C R V N O O B A T S
T C R Y A R C L U E B R Q D
I T I O N E P U Z Z L E S Y
C A R D S H U F F L E F I L
```

Solution on Page 263

AUTOMATIC	METAL
BACK	OPEN
BUILDING	ORNATE
CAR	OUT
CLOSE	PAINT
COLOR	PATIO
DECORATIVE	PORTAL
ENTER	PRIVACY
EXIT	ROOM
FRAME	SECURITY
FRONT	SHUT
GARAGE	SILL
GLASS	SLAM
HANDLE	SLIDING
HINGE	STOP
HOME	SWING
INTERIOR	WINDOW
JAMB	WOOD
KEY	
KNOB	
LIGHT	
LOCK	

```
C R R K E A V E X I T G Z T
M O O R Y I G K O S N P U N
A P L C T N G M W R I O Y U
L E Q O I T A F O W A R T E
S N D W R E R R D O P T U F
M M S E U R A O N O R A H I
C V O M C I G N I D I L S X
B T R O E O E T W R V D S B
O M N H S R R H E M A R F J
N E A U T O M A T I C C M H
K T T J E Z G N T O Y N Q D
C H E G G N I D L I U B H D
O G N S S S A L G T V R E E
L I T K O F M E T A L E C I
H L E S I L L Q Y P O T S C
H Y R E H K C A B K Q G P S
```

Solution on Page 264

BABIES	JOGGER
BALL	KIDS
BEACH	LAKE
BENCH	PARENTS
BIKES	PAVILION
BROOK	PEOPLE
CARNIVAL	PIGEONS
CAROUSEL	POND
CHILDREN	POOL
CHIPMUNK	RIVER
CONCERT	SHOW
CREEK	SLIDE
DADS	SQUIRREL
DEER	SWAN
DOG	SWING
DUCKS	TRAIL
FISH	TREE
FLOWERS	TURTLE
GAME	
GARDEN	
GAZEBO	
GEESE	

```
E G P E I N A W S E G O D Q
H T E C J S L D P H G N K X
U R C W S L I D E A O X L K
T A I O T K N U M P I H C S
G I E V N N L E K B E A C H
P L L K E C H I L D R E N O
D E T D R R E S G N G U B W
D X R G A Z H R I A S D A D
Z A U E P P H V T F Z R L E
G S T E Y C A R O U S E L L
N K A S N L P V R E R G B P
I C R E E K A L I R H G P O
W U B I K E S B I L N O O E
S D E E R V A U V E I J O P
A K O O R B Q S R E W O L F
O C F B Q S N O E G I P N O
```

Solution on Page 264

ANGLE

APPRENTICE

BEVEL

BOX

BUILD

CABINET

CARVE

CHISEL

CONSTRUCT

CUT

DRILL

FINISH

FURNITURE

GLUE

GOGGLES

HAMMER

HANDYMAN

HOUSE

JOINT

LATHE

LEVEL

MASTER

MEASURE

MITER

MOLDING

NAIL

PARQUETRY

PLANE

ROUTER

SAW

SCREW

SKILLED

SQUARE

SUPPORTS

TOOLS

TRADE

TRIM

WALLS

WOOD

WORKSHOP

```
P L A N E R E S B R Q C S I
Y E U S J T R R R E T S A M Y
S S C K R G A T V L W S R E
F I N I S H U D E O G T L U
S H M L T O Q T L C E G P L
F C S L R N S C B U N E O G
O A L E G X E U Q A F R H G
W R O D F S T R O P P U S N
E V O L O U A T P T A S K I
R E T I M P R S E P M A R D
C D N A M Y D N A H A E O L
S A I N L R I O I X O M W O
L R O F I B T C L T C U X M
L T J L A U U D L I U B S K
A O L C E T H A M M E R O E
W O O D L E V E L A T H E X
```

Solution on Page 264

ACADEMIC

ACCOUNTING

ACHIEVEMENT

ART

ASSOCIATE

BACHELOR

BUSINESS

CERTIFICATE

COMMERCE

COMPUTING

CREDENTIALS

DANCE

DESIGN

DIPLOMA

EDUCATION

ENGINEERING

EXPENSIVE

GRADUATE

HISTORY

HONORS

JOURNALISM

LAW

MAJOR

MATHEMATICS

NURSING

PHILOSOPHY

PSYCHOLOGY

SCIENCE

STUDY

TECHNOLOGY

UNIVERSITY

```
N U R S I N G R A D U A T E
E D E S I G N I T U P M O C
C A R L U N I V E R S I T Y
R N O S C I T A M E H T A M
E C J O U R N A L I S M B P
M E A A A A E U Y D U T S H S
M T M S A E O H E X L I T Y
O A B S M N C I V A L E E C
C C A O O I C S I O E D C H
I I C C L G A T S H C U H O
M F H I P N N O N O N C N L
E I E A I E P R E N E A O O
D T L T D H I Y P O I T L G
A R O E Y W A L X R C I O Y
C E R B U S I N E S S O G P
A C H I E V E M E N T N Y T
```

Solution on Page 264

ACTION

AUTHOR

AWARDS

BELLA

BLOOD

BOOK

CHARACTERS

CRAZE

CULLEN

ECLIPSE

EDWARD

FANS

FICTION

FORKS

FOUR

FRANCHISE

GIRLS

HORROR

INTEREST

JACOB

JAMES

LOVE

MEYER

MOVIE

MYSTERIOUS

NEW MOON

NOVEL

PLOT

POPULAR

READING

ROMANCE

SAGA

SCHOOL

TEENS

TWILIGHT

VAMPIRE

WASHINGTON

WEREWOLF

WOLVES

YOUNG ADULT

```
N R S K F K O O B L P N Y W
O E C L I P S E O L E Y P O
V A H C C E R V O L O M P L
E D O R T D E T L U Y O P V
L I O A I W T U N S B V D E
L N L Z O A C G T E O I I S
T G Z E N R A E L W C E M D
K W Q F S D R L A S A W E R
I K I N U I A S S A J E Y A
N N H L O E H P N G C R E W
E H T U I I C C O A K E R A
W O S E N G T N N P F W I U
M R N G R H H C A A U O P T
O R T S N E E T A M R L M H
O O G I R L S S K R O F A O
N R S E M A J T F O U R V R
```

Solution on Page 265

BABY FOOD

BABY OIL

BATH

BIB

BLANKET

BOOTIES

BOTTLE

BRUSH

BURPING

CAR SEAT

CLOTHES

CRADLE

CRAWLING

CRIB

CRYING

DADDY

DIAPERS

FIRST TOOTH

FORMULA

LOTION

LULLABY

MILK

MOMMY

NAPTIME

OINTMENT

PACIFIER

PICTURES

PREGNANT

RASH

RATTLE

SHAMPOO

SLEEP

SOCKS

STROLLER

SWADDLE

TALK

TEDDY BEAR

TEETHING

WALKING

WIPES

```
W A L K I N G N I Y R C P W
I R A S H F O R M U L A V P
P H S E H T O L C B C M T I
E L T T O B U R P I N G E C
S L I O Y B A B F P Y T K T
W C D C O W M I L K E A N U
A P R A L T E D D Y B E A R
D R K I R R T S O C K S L E
D E N P B C H S U R B R B S
L G A R E L L O R T S A B Y
E N P T N E M T N I O C O D
R A T T L E B A B Y F O O D
G N I H T E E T A L K B T A
F T M O M M Y S R E P A I D
L D E S Y B A L L U L T E B
N O I T O L O O P M A H S D
```

Solution on Page 265

APARTMENT

ATTIC

BEACH

BEDROOM

BELONGINGS

BUILD

CABIN

CASTLE

CLOSET

CONDO

COTTAGE

DEN

DOORS

DUPLEX

FAMILY

FARM

FLOORS

FURNITURE

GARAGE

HOUSE

KITCHEN

LARGE

LAWN

LODGE

MANSION

MOBILE

MOTOR

NEW

OFFICE

OLD

PANTRY

PLAN

RANCH

RENTAL

SAFETY

SHACK

SMALL

SWEET

TOWNHOME

YARD

```
Y A R D H F B R E N T A L R
T N W A L A E U C N P V O A
E G A O K M R U I U J T N N
F A O C T I U L F L O U O C
A R P O U L T G F M D L I H
S A A T A Y I C O N D O S H
I G N T F A N O H X D G N C
Q E T A P A R T M E N T A A
E I R G L D U E M I N S M E
C M Y E E P F O G I T Y H B
E Y N B V E H N B L E B O D
S G W E Z N O A E D S N U L
W A D L W L C O L D O P S L
E H E O E L I B O M L O E A
E D T B L L A R G E C D R M
T L V N M J V C X K C A H S
```

Solution on Page 265

ANTIVIRUS

COMPUTER

DAMAGE

DATA

DELETE

DETECTION

DOCUMENTS

DOWNLOAD

FILE

FIREWALL

HARD DRIVE

HARMFUL

HIDDEN

INFECT

INTERNET

MALWARE

NORTON

PROBLEM

PROGRAM

PROTECT

REBOOT

RECOVERY

REGISTRY

REINSTALL

REPRODUCTION

RESIDENT

RESTORE

RISK

SCAN

SOFTWARE

SPAM

SPYWARE

STEALTH

SYMPTOMS

VULNERABILITY

```
V L L A T S N I E R S C A N
D U N S N E I N T E R N E T
A S L T P T V D E L E T E R
T T R N D Y I I R I P O F E
A E I E E I W V R F R O I S
S A S M T R N A I D O B R T
Y L K U E U A F R R D E E O
M T Y C C N P B E E U R W R
P H R O T N O M I C C S A E
T N E D I S E R O L T O L H
O S V O O B D D T C I F L A
M D O W N L O A D O O T L R
S T C E T O R P M I N W Y M
P R E G I S T R Y A H A Y F
A E R A W L A M J B G R C U
M A R G O R P R O B L E M L
```

Solution on Page 265

BALMY

BEACH

BIKING

BOATING

BREEZE

CALM

CHILLY

CLEAR

CLOUDS

COMFORTABLE

CONCERT

CONVERTIBLE

COOL

DEW

FAVORABLE

FISHING

FORECAST

GRILLING

HIKING

LIGHT JACKET

LIGHT SHOWERS

MILD

MIST

PICNIC

POOL

PREDICTABLE

SAILING

SEASONS

SHORTS

SKIING

SNOW FLURRIES

SPRINGTIME

SPRINKLING

SWIMSUIT

TANK TOP

WARM

```
P E L B A T C I D E R P L D
S F F O R E C A S T R O H S
N E B B I K I N G M I S T P
O L R A E C B O A T I N G O
S B E L B A R O V A F O F T
A A E M P J C L E A R W I K
E T Z Y O T T H W E D F S N
S R E W O H S T H G I L H A
A O M D L G S W I M S U I T
I F I G R I L L I N G R N T
L M L A C L O U D S X R G R
I O D O S P R I N G T I M E
N C O N V E R T I B L E R C
G L G N I L K N I R P S A N
C I N C I P G N I K I H W O
V R G N I I K S Y L L I H C
```

Solution on Page 266

ASPHALT

BIG RIGS

BRAKE

BUS

CAR

COMMUTE

CRUISE

CURVES

EXIT

FAST

GAS STATION

INTERSTATE

JAM

LANE

LIGHTS

LINES

MEDIAN

MOTORCYCLES

PASS

PAVEMENT

PLAZAS

RAMP

RIDE

ROADS

ROUTE

SCENERY

SERVICE

SHOULDER

SIGNS

SLOW

SPEED

STEER

STOP

TOLL

TOURIST INFO

TRAFFIC

TRUCKS

TURNS

VEHICLE

YIELD

```
H Z Q E B Y E T U M M O C B
O P L C Y X E Y H G F J U Y
A L L I N D R M B N E X I T
S I O V I E G O I A Y E R S
P G T R N L A T G I L B O L
H H L E T C S O R D S N U O
A T C S E I S R I E I P T W
L S A B R H T C G M G A E R
T F R U S E A Y S P N S K A
R N O X T V T C H L S S A C
A T E S A F I L O A E U R N
F U R M T D O E U Z N U B B
F R A U E O N S L A I M A J
I N M E C V P I D S L A N E
C S P Q H K A S E V R U C P
U S R E E T S P R O A D S G
```

Solution on Page 266

ADVICE	HUSBAND
BEGINNING	JOY
BLISS	LIFE
BRIDE	LOVE
CELEBRATION	MARRIED
CEREMONY	MATE
CERTIFICATE	NEW
CHANGE NAME	PAL
COHORT	PEER
COMRADE	RECEPTION
CONTENT	RINGS
COUPLE	ROMANCE
DEVOTION	SPOUSE
FLIRTY	TOGETHER
FRIEND	UNITED
FUTURE	VACATION
GIFTS	VOWS
GROOM	WIFE
HAPPY	
HELPER	
HITCHED	
HOUSE	

```
Y P P A H D N A B S U H T E
T B B R I D E I R R A M S F
R N E A G A D V I C E Q G I
I E E G E R Y E O N N I N W
L W T T I Y O V H T O O I S
F L A P N N J O E C I N R T
P M C C J O N L M T T O S F
E O I O C M C I A T P I N I
E J F M O E H R N O E T H G
R K I R U R B C E G C A E H
L F T A P E E O G E E C L O
I R R D L C S H N T R A P U
F I E E E W U O A H U V E S
E E C N A M O R H E T G R E
U N I T E D P T C R U O N A
F D V O W S S I L B F O A T
```

Solution on Page 266

BLACK

BOX

CARDS

CHICKEN FOOT

COMPETITION

COUNT

DECK

DESIGN

DIE

DOTS

DOUBLES

DRAW

EFFECT

ENDS

FACE

FALL

FAMILY

FUN

GAME

IVORY

MARBLE

MATH

PACK

PIECES

PIPS

PLAY

POINTS

RECTANGLE

RULES

SCORE

SET

SPINNER

SPOTS

STOCK

STRATEGY

SUITS

TABLE

TILE

TOPPLE

WHITE

Play Dominoes

```
M N H H P L Z G P U M C K J
D D O U B L E S T N U O C A
J C H I C K E N F O O T A M
Z G Y L T I L E U A P C P G
F G Z G D I O U M F C P Q D
S S P R E C T A N G L E L I
L T A D N T Y E S T I U S E
H W O F G L A C P O I N T S
L C S P I P O R D M T S E T
S F A M S R J B T S O E S S
G E A R E N N I P S K C E D
J F L L D F W W H I T E C N
M Y B U L S F Y R O V I B E
A A M A R B L E M A G P L N
T L H O X C A K C A L B O X
H P E D C Z K C O T S T O D
```

Solution on Page 266

AIR

BEACH

BREEZE

CALM

CLEAN

COFFEE

COLD

COOL

DEW

DIP

DRINK

ENLIVEN

EXERCISE

FRUIT

HAMMOCK

HUGS

HUMOR

ICE

INSPIRE

JOG

MILKSHAKE

MINTY

NAPPING

NATURE

NEW

OCEAN

PERFUME

POOL

REVIVE

SHOWER

SMILE

SMOOTHIE

SODA

SPLASH

STORM

SWEETS

SWIM

TEA

TRAVEL

VACATION

```
T J G A E R B N K H A M M S
W R E D N I A N F R U I T S
W O R X E A N E V I L N E V
E M U F R E P W T K K T C S
P U T K E R I P S N I Y H H
S H A S R C K H I M R O T S
P M N L E V A R T N W U S L
J E L N J K D E W E G B B Y
Q H V J E S I C R E X E E N
V H A I J Z N O I T A C A V
Y N N M V S E H P E Z E C N
M L A C M E T E W O L W H M
M C E D F O R E R C O I M I
H P C F O D C J E B O L M W
M X O M I S Z K O W C L W S
Z C S P L A S H U G S D D B
```

Solution on Page 267

ANTENNAS

BIRDS

CABLE

CLIMB

COAXIAL

COMPANY

CONCRETE

CURRENT

ELECTRIC

ENERGY

EQUIPMENT

GRID

HEIGHT

INSULATED

LIGHTS

LINE

MAINTENANCE

OUTSIDE

OVERHEAD

PINE

POLE

POST

POWER

REPAIR

ROAD

ROUND

SAFETY

SERVICE

SHOCK

STEEL

STREET

STRONG

SUBSTATION

SUPPORT

TELEGRAPH

UTILITIES

VOLTAGE

WIRE

WOOD

WORKER

```
U S H O C K T S O P O W E R
V M L F C L I M B W I R E I
L C I H E I G H T S M N M A
C O G O V E R H E A D A E P
P O M H S U B S T A T I O N E
A P T N E T E R C N O C V R
X A S E S I N S T E E L O P
I N S U L A T E D D L N L S
A Y S Q C E N I M R I E T E
L E T E T A G N L P I R A R
Y G R E N E B R E I I B G V
T N E C E I E L A T T U E I
E O E G R K L P E P N U Q C
F R T T R O P P U S H A F E
A T V O U T S I D E W O O D
S S W Y C D N U O R O A D N
```

Solution on Page 267

ANNUITY

BILLS

CHARITIES

CHECK

DONATE

DRAWING

FORTUNE

FRIENDS

GAMBLE

HAPPY

HOUSE

INVEST

JACKPOT

LOTTO

LUCKY

MILLIONAIRE

MONEY

NUMBERS

PAPER

PAYMENT

PAYOUT

PICK

PLAY

POOL

PRIZE

REDEEM

RETIREMENT

RICH

SAVE

SCRATCH

SHARE

SHOPPING SPREE

SPEND

SUM

TAX

TICKET

TRUST

WEALTHY

WILL

WINNER

Solution on Page

```
T E V A S H C I R M O N E Y
R T N E M Y A P Q E G L K D
U S M U S Y T L T P N C O U
S E E P M I F O R T U N E W
T V E L C B P O J L A E I W
G N D K B K E P D T R L L W
D I E U C M B R E P L R A Y
P T R A U T A I S K P E H V
L A J S O W U G L Q C T F H
A X E R I A N O I L L I M C
Y A N N U I T Y Y A S R P T
E K G Y P T J D E A X E A A
R C C P O X Y W Z S P M X R
A E O P C H A R I T I E S C
H H P A P E R F R I E N D S
S C Y H O U S E P L G T I Y
```

Solution on Page 267

BED
BLANKET
CASE
CHAIR
COMFORT
COUCH
COVER
DECOR
DESIGN
DOWN
DREAM
FEATHER
FIGHT
FIRM
FLUFFY
FOAM
HARD
HEAD
HYPOALLERGENIC
KING
LACE
LINEN

NAP
NECK
NIGHT
ORTHOPEDIC
POLYESTER
QUEEN
RELAX
REST
SATIN
SILK
SLEEP
SLIP
SOFA
STUFFING
THROW
TOP
TRAVEL
WHITE

Solution on P.

```
U C B Z O R T H O P E D I C
Y P I L S X A T M O Q L C I
X X Z N A R G S M L P D T N
E K D L D N X E L Y R X H E
F M E A W K K R D E C O R G
R R H O E E T E A S E G O R
Y I D W K H R M T T O P W E
Q F N H G I O U R E V O C L
I K L I S A F O S R H K B L
U M F T L F M L B C I F E A
N N P E I E O O U N A V D O
E I I N N A C O G F A S N P
E T G U E T C I E R F D E Y
U A O H N H S G T C O Y C H
Q S D U T E L B R P A N K F
M J T Y D R I A H C M L G U
```

Solution on Page 267

ADDRESS

BILLS

BOX

BUBBLE WRAP

BULK

CANCELLED

CARD

CERTIFIED

CLASS

CLERKS

COUNTER

DELIVER

ENVELOPE

FORMS

GIFTS

INSURE

INVITATIONS

LABEL

LETTER

LINE

MAIL

METER

MONEY ORDER

NOTIFY

PACKAGE

PARCELS

PASSPORT

PEOPLE

POSTAGE

PURCHASE

RECEIVE

SCALE

SEND

SHIP

SORT

STAMPS

TAPE

TRACKING

TRUCKS

USPS

```
K S G I F T S G S S H B L D
L E B A L K N M S P R I E W
U S P S R I R E A O N L V E
B A K E K O R R L E I L I U
A H L C F D C E C V S S E L
N C A R D E L L E C N A C I
O R S A L A E R M R O P E A
T U K S C E P A T E I E R M
I P A S S P O R T D T O T E
F A B U B B L E W R A P I T
Y C O U N T E R O O T L F E
L K X T D T V S S Y I E I R
A A E R U S N I H E V E E Y
J G L E T T E R I N N C D J
D E G A T S O P P O I D B Z
Z T R U C K S T A M P S D G
```

Solution on Page 268

ACCESSORIES

BEAUTY

BRAND

CLOTH

COLORS

COSTUME

COUTURE

CREATE

CUT

DESIGN

DRESS

FAD

HAT

HEM

HOT

INDUSTRY

JEANS

LACE

LATEST

LEGGINGS

LENGTH

MATERIAL

MODEL

NEW

PANTS

PARIS

PATTERN

POPULAR

RUNWAY

SCARF

SEW

SHIRT

SILK

SKIRT

STORES

STYLE

TAILOR

TREND

VOGUE

WEAR

```
E T T S T J T D Y R S S R Q
O X S D K L E N N T P I A G
L M H T E I E E O A U R C B
J U Z N O S R R T T B A C I
C S G W F R I T S A N P E X
S T N A P L E G G I N G S B
H Y D D A R I S N L C S S T
H L W T N M C H T O L C O U
R E E P S A A O U R S H R A
N S M S L Y R T S U D N I R
T S E E G A U B E T C S E A
Q R D K L R H J S R U L S E
D O A U E N H E E I I M C W
M L P R U N W A Y H L A E I
V O G U E H T N T S L K L B
P C U T Q E V S C A R F I H
```

Solution on Page 268

BOIL

BRAISE

BURNER

COOK

DINNER

EGGS

FIRE

FOOD

FRY

GRIDDLE

GRILLED CHEESE

HEAT

HOT

KETTLE

LADLE

LUNCH

MACARONI

MEAT

OMELET

PANS

PASTA

PEPPER

POT

RECIPES

RICE

SALT

SAUCE

SEAR

SIMMER

SKILLET

SOUP

SPATULA

SPILLS

SPLATTER

STEAM

STIR

TIMER

VEGETABLES

WARM

WATER

```
G U F M K E T T L E S A L T
P R S P E E V W L G B R Q M
F E I E L A O S G U E C I R
G S P L A T T E R N N X I A
Z B I P L R L N N I G C O W
S K K L E E E I A M R P H T
S P D A U R D X A E I U A D
R C I D K O O C M O D O O F
M E T L N I A M H E D S Z R
A O C E L R I P E E L R S Y
E H P I O S A U C E E P O T
T S Y N P N R T S T A S M T
S B I S S E L B A T E G E V
N A O A M A S W U E I Y L K
M E F I R E D L T O H R E M
Z T T V L B A T S A P T T X
```

Solution on Page 268

BATH

BEACH

BIKINI

BOATS

BUBBLES

CANOEING

DIVE

FLIPPERS

FLOAT

FLUME

GAMES

GOGGLES

HOSE

JACUZZI

KAYAKING

LAZINESS

LESSONS

LIFEGUARD

NOODLES

OCEAN

PADDLE

POOL

RACE

RELAXATION

SAILING

SCUBA GEAR

SLIDE

SNORKEL

SOAKED

SPLASH

SPRAY

SQUIRT GUN

STROKE

SUNSCREEN

SUNSHINE

SURFING

SWIM

TUBING

WATER

WAVES

```
G E W S P G N I E O N A C R
D D N O O D L E S S O N S E
O I O A J A C U Z Z I J D C
N L V K S U P O K F T R N A
W S S E N I Z A L W A T E R
A E E D O B Y O D U X R E I
V L M F R A A P G D A F R N
E G A L K T I E O E L M C I
S G G I E H F C G H E E S K
T O N P L I E A F I R U N I
R G I P L A B S E L B B U B
O B L E N U G T R I U Q S B
K E I R C H S A L P S M X O
E A A S U N S H I N E Y E A
H C S U R F I N G N I B U T
C H O S E S W I M Y A R P S
```

Solution on Page 268

AXLE	PEDAL
BALANCE	PERFORMANCE
CHAIN	RIDE
CIRCUS	SADDLE
CLOWNS	SAFETY
CRANK	SEAT
CYCLE	SHOW
DIFFICULT	SINGLE
ELBOW PADS	SKILL
FALL	SPOKE
FESTIVAL	STUNT
FRAME	TALL
FREESTYLE	TIRE
FUN	TOY
GIRAFFE	TRICK
HEIGHT	UPRIGHT
HELMET	VEHICLE
HOBBY	WHEEL
JUGGLE	
LEGS	
MUNI	
PARADE	

```
R A E M A R F V P T P L Z D
S S X K N A R C N A E R I T
G S A L T P E C I E R F U N
E I D F E P E I A S F A U L
L N R D E T S R H I O P D E
E G A A R T T C C P R M S E
T L S I F O Y U I I M D I H
N E C K Y F L S G F A L L W
U K V Y I T E H T P N E I M
T S W B C L T S W W C C U T
S H R I D E L O T F E N J A
W O G D H O B B Y I I A U L
B W A I C L O W N S V L G L
N S Q V E H I C L E Q A G N
T M Y R X H E L M E T B L P
R E J F M D H W S P O K E N
```

Solution on Page 269

AGE

BITTERSWEET

CARDS

CHARMING

CHILDHOOD

DESIRE

DIARY

DWELL

EVENTS

FEELING

FOND

FRIENDS

GENERATION

HANDKERCHIEF

HAPPINESS

HOMESICK

JEWELRY

KEEPSAKES

LACE

MEMORIES

MOVIES

OLD

RECALL

REFLECTIVE

REMEMBER

REMINISCENT

RETRO

SENTIMENTAL

SOUVENIR

TOKEN

TRADITION

WEDDING DRESS

YESTERYEAR

```
S E K A S P E E K N E K O T
U S E I R O M E M O V I E S
K G E V I T C E L F E R L D
C H A R M I N G F W Q A W O
I H A N D K E R C H I E F O
S C R S Y G J E W E L R Y H
E A N M C A N M I L G E R D
M R O S E N T I M E N T A L
O D I F R I E N D S I R E I
H S T N E V E I K D L O Y H
Y B I T T E R S W E E T R C
R V D J L L A C E R E W E S
A H A P P I N E S S F F T G
I T R C L R I N E V U O S E
D F T W N O I T A R E N E G
R E M E M B E R I S E D Y A
```

Solution on Page 269

BACKWARDS

BALANCE

BLADES

BOARD

CIRCLES

COMPETITION

DERBY

DOWNHILL

EXERCISE

FALL

FIGURE

FITNESS

GOAL

HELMET

HOCKEY

ICE

INDOOR

INLINE

JUMPS

PADS

PAIRS

PARK

PIPE

PROFESSIONAL

PUCK

RACING

RAMP

RECREATION

RINK

ROAD

ROLLER

ROUTINE

SIDEWALK

SLALOM

SNOW

SPEED

SPINS

SPORT

TOUR

WHEELS

```
X T K N I R W C I R C L E S
A O G G O A L I B L A D E S
P U P G N I C A R N E W P P
P R N B R E T S O R K Z A M
R M Q O O M Y I U D S A D U
L O A A L F S G T E N H S J
E L A R L S I E E E I E L E
S C A D E F D T C P P L A X
R D R F R C I R N S S M L E
I T O R W T R N A E P E O R
A R U W O O H E L W S T M C
P O T K N O N Y A I K S K I
E P I P C H D S B T N C R S
A S N K C U I N C R I E A E
W H E E L S P L I B E O P B
M Y S I D E W A L K Q D N D
```

Solution on Page 269

ANACONDA

BASILISK

BEHEMOTH

BIGFOOT

CENTAUR

CTHULHU

DEMON

DEVIL

DINOSAUR

DRAGON

FOLKLORE

GARGOYLE

GIANT

GNOME

GOBLIN

GODZILLA

GORGON

GRIFFIN

HYDRA

IMP

KRAKEN

LEGEND

MINOTAUR

MUMMY

MUTANT

MYSTICAL

NESSIE

OGRE

PREDATOR

SATYR

SCARY

SERPENT

SIREN

SNAKE

TERROR

TROLL

VAMPIRE

WEREWOLF

YETI

ZOMBIE

```
E K A N S P R E D A T O R Y
E G O R G O N I L B O G O M
V A M P I R E L I V E D H M
D Z N I F F I R G V R B Y U
T E P F M Z L Y O U P A D M
N E M L D I C A A L N S R E
A I I O I I N T C A K I A R
T S G W N T N O C I Q L G G
U S B E H E M O T H T I O O
M E I R C Y N U S A D S N F
Z N G E R D H E D A U K Y R
O E F W A L R N V M U R O M
M R O X U P E L Y O G R A G
B I O H E G I A N T R O L L
I S T N E K A R K E M O N G
E C T L W R S A T Y R A C S
```

Solution on Page 269

BEVERAGE

BOTTLE

BUBBLY

CAN

CHERRY

CITRUS

CLEAR

COKE

COLA

CRISP

DIET

DRINK

FANTA

FATTENING

FIZZY

FLAVOR

FOUNTAIN

GINGER ALE

GLASS

GRAPE

ICED

LEMON

LIME

ORANGE

PEPSI

POP

QUENCHING

ROOT BEER

SERVE

SPARKLING

SPRITE

STRAW

SUGAR

SWEET

SYRUP

TASTY

TINGLY

TREAT

VANILLA

WATER

```
X M F W A R T S E R V E G H
G S I S P E P R S A L O C T
Q E Z G O W R E U E E Q N R
R M Z F P K N E R L M G I E
L R Y L B B U B T C O N A A
Q E R A E J Q T I A N I T T
V F R V M L O O C N W L N E
R R E O I B A O Q S M K U E
N S H R L S Y R U P S R O W
R V C A G N I N E T T A F S
K F A N T A D T N G Y P L U
T E G N A R O A C R N S P G
C E E T I R P S H A Y I T A
K T I N G L Y T I P U R G R
K B K D P R L Y N E I C E D
M Y B E V E R A G E K O C B
```

Solution on Page 270

AND	NOT
AWAY	PAT
BAT	PEG
BIG	PIG
BOY	PLAY
COT	POT
DIG	RAT
DOG	READ
FATHER	RIG
FUN	ROT
GIRL	RUN
GIVE	SAT
HAT	SEE
HELP	SIT
HOG	SKY
JUMP	THIS
LITTLE	TOP
LOT	YOURS
MAT	
MITT	
MOP	
NET	

```
X B W Q H P R P M S K L V R
A N P Y N Q V O C I G I V E
H C T Z G E P T T H T T L H
V J N O T I Y O B T Q T K T
W M B D G X Z P D I T O O A
O H E M N B O L R I G C F F
G O B P V Z K E L O O I J L
E P X M U A E H H P D S D J
Y H O T D X E E E T M R I N
H U R K Y Y N U R B L U I T
N D A L A Z S A K U O O J G
C Q G G F N T A P L A Y T E
A K A G V A O H R E A D E O
A I L Y S K Y T A W N S N K
U O W H Q A Q B A T D U Z Z
C P U O H R T R Q M Y Q F V
```

Solution on Page 270

ADVERTISING

ARTICLE

AUDIENCE

BBC

BIAS

BROADCAST

BULLETIN

CABLE

CNN

COMMUNICATION

COVERAGE

CURRENT

ECONOMY

EDITOR

ENTERTAINMENT

EVENTS

FOX

GOSSIP

GOVERNMENT

IMPORTANT

INTERNET

JOURNALISM

LOCAL

MAGAZINE

MEDIA

NBC

ONLINE

PAPER

POLITICS

PRINT

PUBLIC

RADIO

REPORT

SPORTS

STORY

TELEVISION

VIEW

WAR

WEATHER

```
C O V E R A G E N I L N O D
O S T N E V E E L C I T R A
M P M N H T S E R O T I D E
M R A J T N E M N R E V O G
U I G P A E A U D I E N C E
N N A O E R A W I R L J B O
I T Z L W R N B T T B O A I
C E I C O U B I T E A U I D
A R N N B C S S T L C R D A
T N E M N I A T R E T N E R
I E R W N C A L D V L A M C
O T E G D G O S S I P L S I
N I P A S T R O P S X I U L
V F O X P O L I T I C S E B
Z R R O T N A T R O P M I U
B S T O R Y Y M O N O C E P
```

Solution on Page 270

AIR	LIGHT
BAG	LOUD
CANISTER	MACHINE
CARPET	MOTOR
CLEAN	NOISE
CORD	NOZZLE
CYCLONE	PLUG
CYLINDER	PORTABLE
DIRT	PUMP
DUST	PUSH
DYSON	ROBOTIC
ELECTRIC	ROOM
EUREKA	RUG
FILTER	SUCK
FLOOR	TOOLS
HANDLE	UPRIGHT
HARDWOOD	WET
HEAVY	WHEELS
HOME	
HOOVER	
HOSE	
HOUSE	

```
D A G F V T H G I L R H J V
Z K M I D H O O V E R O T P
O E R L Y G M O T O R U O F
R R E T S I N A C E B S O M
Q U D E O R D L L N A E L C
J E N R N P H B H I G S S W
Y T I T U U A A C H K I Q H
Z E L E C T R I C C H O M E
X P Y W R D T D Y A F N L E
T R C O W O A U C M B Z G L
F A P O B I P O L M Z T U S
M C O O R N F L O O R O L L
K D R M P D H A N D L E P B
T C I X F U O H E A V Y U A
E G U R I P S T V K C L M A
D D U S T Z E H I A R B P S
```

Solution on Page 270

ACCESSORY

ASCOT

BOW

CASUAL

CLIP

CLOTH

COLOR

CRAVAT

DAD

DESIGN

DOTS

DRESS

EVENT

FABRIC

FANCY

GIFT

JACKET

KNOT

LONG

MEN

NECK

OFFICE

PAISLEY

PATTERN

PIN

POLYESTER

PRESENT

PROFESSIONAL

RACK

SHIRT

SILK

STRIPE

STYLE

SUIT

TIE

TUX

WEAR

WIDE

WINDSOR

WORK

```
K C K W I D E J M F M C Q P
P L G G S X R T T N E V E P
Z X I Z F H D E S G S T O D
L S F A F W I T S I J L B W
O A T V F A R R N S Y J F P
N K N R H K N O T E K C A J
G L L O I C F C S D S W M A
V B V I I P A T Y D T E S P
U Y R O S S E C C A N C R W
K W D T U R S C Y O O I G P
R G Y A F N R E T T A P W K
A L L R D A L O F F I C E Z
E I X J V S B C L O T H I H
W U U A I U P R W O R K T Z
O B T A A I C L I P C P G Q
B F P U N T I N E C K C A R
```

ARROWS

BE MINE

BOUQUETS

CAKE

CANDY

CARDS

COOKIE

CRUSHES

CUPS

DECORATIONS

DOILIES

EXCHANGE

FAMILY

FAVORS

FESTIVE

FLOWERS

FOOD

FORKS

FRIEND

FUN

GAMES

GARLAND

GIFT

HEART

HUGS

INVITATIONS

KISSES

LOVE

NAPKINS

PINK

PLATES

PRIZES

RED

RIBBON

ROMANCE

ROSES

SPOONS

SWEETS

VALENTINES

WHITE

```
G S N O I T A R O C E D R P
W A N S W O R R A X E V O L
T H R O V F O E C A R D S A
B K I L I M A H D F C B E T
E I Z T A T A M O T A V S E
P S S N E N A O I F N A S S
I S C P G V D T L L D L T E
N E C E O Q I O I S Y E E H
K S P U C O W T E V U N E S
C G F R I E N D S Q N T W U
F A V O R S K S U E U I S R
O M U S E I K O O C F N U C
R E R Z T M B E N I M E B A
K S I F N N A P K I N S B K
S R I B B O N H E A R T R E
P G J O S G U H U K P P W R
```

Solution on Page 271

ABACUS

ADD

ALGEBRA

ANGLES

AREA

CALCULUS

COMPUTE

COSINE

COUNT

DECIMAL

DIFFERENCE

DIGITS

DIVIDE

EQUALS

FACTOR

FIGURES

FINITE

FORMULA

FRACTION

GEOMETRY

GRAPHING

MATHEMATICS

MONEY

MULTIPLE

NEGATIVE

NUMBERS

NUMERAL

POSITIVE

PRIME

PRODUCT

QUOTIENT

RATIO

ROOT

SETS

SOLVE

SUM

TANGENT

TRIGONOMETRY

VECTOR

```
S V C O U N T N E G N A T P
L S O L V E F O R M U L A O
A E N I S O C U I D F G D S
U L T C U D O R P T R E D I
Q G R A P H I N G H A B Y T
E N E L A M I C E D C R E I
T A S C I T A M E H T A M V
I N D U N V F R F E I B I E
N U I L A E R A M B O A R V
I M G U S C R O C F N C P I
F E I S U T N E I T O U Q T
Y R T E M O E G F M O S S A
E A S H G R U S P F T R K G
N L S I O R M U L T I P L E
O O R O E V T D I V I D E N
M T T S R E B M U N U M K W
```

Solution on Page 271

APPLE

BASKETBALL

BISCUITS

BLESSINGS

BOARD GAME

CARD GAME

CARROTS

CIDER

CRANBERRY

DECORATION

EAT

FAMILY

FOOTBALL

FRIENDS

GRACE

GUESTS

NAPS

NOVEMBER

OLIVES

PARADE

PECAN

PIE

PLAY

POTATOES

PRAYERS

PUMPKIN

RELAX

ROLLS

SQUASH

STUFFING

TABLE

TOASTS

TRAYS

TRIMMINGS

TURKEY

TURNIP

VISIT

WALKS

WISHBONE

YAMS

Thanksgiving

```
R O L L S T O R R A C P E S
R E D I C A R D G Z R M D M
E V L L A B T E K S A B A A
N C B P C L S C B G N O R Y
F S A L P E Q O D M B L A F
A O T R E A U R P F E I P R
M S O U G S A A E C R V T I
I P T T F O S T C A R E O E
L P R I B F H I A R Y S A N
Y U O A U A I O N D T T S D
X M S T Y C L N S G I U T S
A P K U A E S L G A S R S U
L K L R L T R I M M I N G S
E I A K P T O S B E V I X J
R N W E S T S E U G S P A N
T R A Y S A W I S H B O N E
```

Solution on Page 271

ADVERTISING

BILLIONAIRE

BOOK CLUB

CALIFORNIA

CEO

CHAIRMAN

COLLEGE

COMPUTER

COURSEMATCH

DAUGHTER

DORMITORY

ENTREPRENEUR

INFLUENTIAL

INTERNET

MANDARIN

MAXIMA

MONEY

MOVIE

NETWORKING

PALO ALTO

PHILANTHROPIST

PRISCILLA CHAN

PROGRAMMER

RICH

ROOMMATES

SETTLEMENT

WEALTH

ZUCK

```
K P N L C R E T U P M O C E
C R A I M O B U L C K O O B
U I M N P A L O A L T O U P
Z C R F M I H O Y J Z B R V
P H I L A N T H R O P I S T
R A A U N R L C O E S L E N
O D H E D O A O T C I L M E
G V C N A F E L I E N I A M
R E M T R I W L M I T O T E
A R A I I L L E R V E N C L
M T X A N A R G O O R A H T
M I I L C C O E D M N I Y T
E S M H D A U G H T E R E E
R I A G N I K R O W T E N S
E N T R E P R E N E U R O Z
O G R O O M M A T E S D M S
```

Solution on Page 272

AGRICULTURE

ASIA

BEET

BOILING

CANE

COMBINE

COOKING

CROP

CUBA

CUTTING

ETHANOL

FIBROUS

FIELD

FOOD

GROW

HARVEST

HAWAII

HEAT

HYBRIDS

INDUSTRY

ISLANDS

JUICE

MACHETE

MILL

MOLASSES

PLANT

PROCESSED

PURE

RAW

REED

REFINE

RUM

SOUTH AMERICA

SPECIES

STOUT

SUGAR

SWEET

TALL

TROPICS

WATER

Sugarcane

```
A S W E E T A L L Q F O O D
Y P R O C E S S E D J T L O
P E X U H S H E C N B E E T
U C X J M A T L U A I S A L
R I E U F E W W T F G F L P
E E T I H C G A T N U I E O
R S H C O N E N I B M O C R
U V A E I H A L N I S P S C
T M N K M L I F G H C D D W
L A O R P O S V T A I F N O
U O L A B W L U S R P I A R
C E Y G Q A O A B V O B L G
I N D U S T R Y S E R R S S
R A W S S E H P E S T O I S
G C U B A R E E D T E U L N
A C I R E M A H T U O S P C
```

Solution on Page 272

ACHIEVE

AFFIRM

ASPIRE

BELIEVE

BRIGHT

CAPABLE

CARING

CHEER

CONFIDENT

CONQUER

DEDICATED

DETERMINED

DREAM

EAGERNESS

ENCOURAGE

EXCELLENT

FUNNY

GOALS

HOPE

IDEALISM

JOY

KIND

LIMITLESS

LOVE

MOTIVATE

OVERCOME

PASSION

PLAN

PROUD

REWARD

STRONG

SUCCESS

SUPPORT

SURE

UPBEAT

UPLIFTING

VISION

WIN

YES

ZEAL

Solution on Page

```
S U C C E S S T R O N G R S
V I S I O N F U N N Y X E G
J E G N I T F I L P U Y W C
O N T K M Z N E L B A P A C
Y C R D R R E E H C C J R L
W O O E I D P A L M H E D I
I U P N F E O G L L I M N M
N R P I F D H E R B E O I I
A A U M A I I R E R V C K T
L G S R L C D N U I E R X L
P E L E S A E E Q G I E U E
R R A T U T A S N H L V P S
O I O E R E L S O T E O B S
U P G D E D I L C L B L E Q
D S N O I S S A P D R E A M
C A R I N G M O T I V A T E
```

Solution on Page 272

BAKE

BANANA

BATTER

BERRIES

BUTTERSCOTCH

CARAMEL

CARROT

CELEBRATE

CHIPS

CHOCOLATE

COLORFUL

DECORATED

EAT

FILLED

FLOUR

FROSTED

FUDGE

ICING

LEMON

MILK

MOCHA

NUTS

ORANGE

OVEN

PARTY

PECAN

PLAIN

PUMPKIN

SERVE

SHARING

SMALL

SPONGE

STRAWBERRY

SUGAR

SWEET

SWIRL

TASTE

VANILLA

WHITE

YELLOW

Cupcakes

```
C T P L R I W S W H I T E T
V W O L L E Y L E M O N K Q
Q Y T R A P A R A G U S S S
F L O U R I O T C A D A B P
N M O C H A N I K P M U P I
Q P G C H O C O L A T E F H
F E E D E C O R A T E D Q C
I C S T R A W B E R R Y E A
L A W N A R S R D V J G W R
L N E U E R S E B A N A N A
E I E T D C B I I A K L I M
D E T S O R F E R R B A K E
T A S T E H C O L O R F U L
B U C Y S P O N G E N E V O
S H A R I N G G N I C I B C
S M A L L I N A V S E R V E
```

Solution on Page 272

PUZZLES • 131

ANIMALS

ART

BALANCE

BLEND

CANVAS

CHALK

CHILDREN

COLORS

CONTENT

CRAYON

CREATIVE

DEPTH

DESIGNS

DEXTERITY

DIMENSIONS

DISTORT

DOODLE

DRAW

ERASER

FORMS

FUN

GRAPHITE

GRID

HUES

IMAGES

INK

MEDIUMS

MIXED MEDIA

OBJECTS

PASTELS

PEN

PICTURE

SCALE

SKETCH

SKILL

SMUDGE

STILL LIFE

SUPPLIES

TECHNIQUES

TRACE

```
O B J E C T S M U D G E G I
S K N I E B A L A N C E G M
J M L Y X V E R A S E R E A
D G R A P H I T E M I D D G
I A W O H O H T Z D I I A E
S G A Z F C U P A U M N P S
T L R M I X E D M E D I A J
O L D D N N S S N L R R S D
R I E N U F T S X A T C T P
T K S E U Q I N H C E T E I
N S I L C O L O R S E R L C
E K G B N D L C A N V A S T
T E N S E I L P P U S C G U
N T S P Y T I R E T X E D R
O C T I P M F X D O O D L E
C H I L D R E N O Y A R C P
```

Solution on Page 273

ALIGN

ARIES

ASTRAL

BIRTH

CANCER

CAPRICORN

CHART

CUSP

DIVINER

EARTH

EQUINOX

FATE

FINANCES

FIRE

FORECAST

FORTUNE

FUTURE

GEMINI

HOROSCOPE

HOUSE

LEO

LIBRA

MERCURY

MONTH

MOON

PATH

PISCES

PLANETS

PREDICT

ROMANCE

SATURN

SCORPIO

SEER

SIGN

SKY

STARS

SUN

TAURUS

VIRGO

WATER

```
N M O N T H O U S E K C H L
F R M O O N Q T A U R U S Y
T I O G O B I R T H T A P R
K O R C F H R F U T U R E U
K I C E I O Y W R W E C O C
V P T F O R T U N E N P N R
T R R S D O P S S A I U E E
Z O A H A S E A C S S C Q M
F C H T Q C G N C T N U T N
M S C R N O E E A A I S K Y
K S T A E P S R M N L P D V
L E N E Z E S O O I S I G N
D I V I N E R X V F N N G Y
F R B A L A R T S A C I J N
Z A Z R E E L K S T L P W M
Z R E T A W O P R E D I C T
```

Solution on Page 273

AROMA

BAG

BLEND

BRAZIL

BREW

CAN

COARSE

CROP

CUP

DARK

DRY

FARM

FILTER

FINE

FLAVOR

FRESH

GOURMET

GRIND

HARVEST

HUSKS

JAVA

LATTE

LIGHT

MEDIUM

MOCHA

ORGANIC

PIT

PLANT

POT

PRESS

PULP

RICH

ROAST

ROBUSTA

SEEDS

SHOP

SOAK

WATER

WEIGHT

WHOLE

```
E P P L A N T H Q V T C J E
P H X B L E N D E O O D P B
A V A J M R H Q U H N O K R
T Z W R E E U E L O H W N X
O S U T V C S P I S Q H O I
R O A X S E K R Z D C T J H
G W R O B U S T A I N H W M
A K A U R R H T R O F G E D
N K C F M S E E B O C I G J
I S D E E S T W C A V L N S
C O T R D L H B D H P A P E
U I F R I P G N O C R T L E
P Z Y F U O I K B O E T U F
J W U N M R E R M M S E P A
O M B A G C W A S J S O V R
L K A C K I D D T H T K G M
```

Solution on Page 273

AMARANTH

ANNIVERSARY

AROMATIC

ARRANGE

BIRTHDAY

BRIDE

CARRY

CASCADING

CATCH

CELEBRATION

COLORFUL

CORSAGE

DAHLIA

DAISY

DATE

FERN

FLORIST

FLOWER

FRESH

GIFT

GREENS

HYDRANGEA

IRIS

LAVENDER

LEAVES

LILAC

NOSEGAY

ORCHID

PEONY

RIBBON

ROSE

SILK

THROW

TOSS

TULIP

VALENTINE

VASE

WATER

WEDDING

WRIST

```
P L Y E G N A R R A C I O W
Z W A R N T S I R O L F O A
C Q D V A I T U L I P R A T
A W H T E S T O R C H I D E
T F T A B N R N S T Y A C R
C A R R Y F D E E S D W E S
H C I E U Y G E V L R Y L I
W D B L S A N Z R I A G E L
E E E R S H O O B G N V B K
J V D R E I P B E I G N R C
A I O D R W O S D P E T A D
I C Y I I N O A E S A L T W
L E S A V N C L O V I N I R
H G I F T S G R F L A R O I
A M A R A N T H G R E E N S
D X D C I T A M O R A F L T
```

Solution on Page 273

BACKPACK

BEACH

BIRD

BOOTS

BUGS

CAMERA

CREEK

DEER

DIRT

EXERCISE

EXPLORE

FERNS

FISH

FLOWER

FOREST

HIKE

HILLS

INSECT

LEAVES

MEADOW

NESTS

OBSERVE

OCEAN

OUTSIDE

PLANTS

POND

PRAIRIE

QUIET

RABBITS

ROCKS

SCENIC

SHAPES

SMELL

SOIL

SOUNDS

SUN

TREE

TWIGS

WINDY

WOODS

```
T D H F O R E S T I B B A R
Q K T I W E A R E M A C N S
Q D I O K K E S I C R E X E
L I O S Z E C P K S W K Z V
Z D Y D R E X P L O R E U A
S G D N Q R A L D B F D N E
G L N U A C I A S S N I U L
I L I O K H E T K E P S S Z
W E W S J M N C S R T T D H
T M E H F A O T A V B U F W
R S C A L R S I N E S O E L
E G M P O B R G A C Q S D P
E U C E W I N S E C T N Q D
J B M S E R I N C O O R E I
G K Y A R D I J O P T E J R
G W B E A C H B A C R F Q T
```

Solution on Page 274

BEER
BUN
CHAIRS
CHIPS
CORN
CUPS
DRINKS
FLAME
FRIENDS
GAS
GRILL
GUESTS
ICE
KEBAB
KETCHUP
MATCHES
MEAT
MUSTARD
NAPKINS
OUTSIDE
PARTY
PATIO

PORK
RELISH
RIBS
ROAST
ROLLS
SALADS
SEATING
SERVE
SMOKE
SNACKS
SODA
SPRING
STEAK
SUMMER
TONGS
TOPPINGS
VEGGIES
YARD

Solution on P

Tasty Barbecue

```
N N B E I S A G R O L L S U
Z R R F R S T N S S V K T G
S I H O U T S I D E C C P Y
C B A M C S N R G A R A G U
Y S M U L D I P N T T V U D
T E P C W A K S E I G G E V
R S W H B L P X O N U B S R
A I P A L A A U T G B D T E
P C B I P S N C H I P S S L
X E R R L D M A T C H E S K
K G V S G N I P P O T C F A
R X X K S E F H S I L E R E
O O Q N O I L K Y N L D K T
P P K I D R A T S U M O V S
H W D R A F M E A T M S W T
Y A R D R E E B D S G N O T
```

Solution on Page 274

ALGAE

ANIMAL

ARCHAEA

BACTERIA

BIOLOGY

BOTANY

CELL

CHROMISTA

CLASS

DIVIDED

DIVISION

DOMAIN

EMPIRES

EUKARYOTIC

FAMILY

FUNGI

GENUS

GROUP

HIERARCHY

HISTORY

KINGDOM

LIFE

LIVING

MONERA

ORGANISM

ORIGIN

PHYLA

PLANT

PROKARYOTIC

PROTISTA

RANK

RESEARCH

SCIENCE

SPECIES

SYSTEM

TAXONOMY

TREE

ZOOLOGY

```
E F I L Y L I M A F U N G I
P R O K A R Y O T I C N S S
S Z O O L O G Y O H I R E M
U S Y S T E M P R V T Y I Y
N M S Y G O L O I B O H H R
E S W P N L M L G D Y C J O
G I W O E I N N I I R R O T
L N X C S C O V N A A A D S
B A C T E R I A R T K E O I
T G A M S D S E C S U S M H
S R L O E P I A S I E E A H
S O G D R H V H P T X R I D
A U A G I Y I C B O T A N Y
L P E N P L D R A R E N O M
C A N I M A L A E P L A N T
R A N K E C N E I C S M U T
```

Solution on Page 274

BAG

BELT

BLANKET

BLAZER

BLOUSE

BOARD GAME

BOOTS

BOXES

CLOTHES

COAT

DRESS

FLATS

GIFTS

GOWN

HANGER

HATS

HEELS

JACKET

JEANS

LIGHT

MITTENS

MONSTER

ORGANIZER

PANTS

PICTURES

PILLOWS

PRESENTS

PURSE

ROD

SHIRT

SHOES

SKIRT

SLACKS

SOCKS

SUIT

SUSPENDERS

SWEATS

TIE

TOOLS

TOWEL

```
U J J V F X G N M F V K S P
S D R E S S N E T T I M I H
T R I H S U L Q H S H L Q S
N B O O T S E H T O L C H K
E B Q V R P G S N O J O Y I
S M L T L E B M W H E D O R
E T A A R N Z S O S A P J T
R D A G Z D B I G N N I A A
P T H H D E U L N A S C C O
A O I E S R R B A A B T K C
N W Y U E S A N O N G U E I
T E O G S L S O A X K R T R
S L N I E A S T B I E E O W
B A H F U C S T A E W S T P
H L U T S K U A V L I G H T
P U R S E S K C O S F T K J
```

Solution on Page 274

BILL POLIAN

CAM NEWTON

CHAMPIONSHIP

CLUB

FANS

GAME

GREG OLSEN

JERSEYS

JOHN FOX

JOHN KASAY

JOSH NORMAN

KAWANN SHORT

KEVIN GREENE

LUKE KUECHLY

MIKE TOLBERT

MORRISON

NFL

PROFESSIONAL

PURRCUSSION

REGGIE WHITE

RON RIVERA

RYAN KALIL

SEASON

SIR PURR

TEAM

THOMAS DAVIS

TITLES

TOPCATS

TRAI TURNER

Carolina Panthers

```
E L A N O I S S E F O R P R
M M Y R E G G I E W H I T E
A S I V A D S A M O H T M N
G N A G N O S A E S K E I R
R O T R O H S N N A W A K U
E T I A E R J O E J S M E T
G W T Y H V I S E O I B T I
O E L A N P I I R H R I O A
L N E S M J F R G N P L L R
S M S A B E A R N F U L B T
E A H K U R N O I O R P E O
N C C N L S S M V X R O R P
Z Y L H C E U K E K U L T C
D P F O R Y A N K A L I L A
A O N J O S H N O R M A N T
P P U R R C U S S I O N S T
```

Solution on Page 275

ANCHOR

BAY

BEACH

BOAT

CANAL

CAPTAIN

CARGO

CLEAT

COAST

COIL

CRANE

FERRY

HARBOR

JETTY

KNOT

LAKE

LAND

LINES

LOADING

MARINA

MOOR

OCEAN

PIER

PORT

REPAIR

RIVER

ROPE

SAIL

SEA

SHIP

SHORE

STERN

TIDE

TRAWLER

TUG

UNLOAD

WHARF

WORKERS

YACHT

YARD

```
M N D Y P Y U I N N S A I L
Y O A F A Q L J L F E G A R
S R O E C B J I J A S N W E
D E B R C O T G N I D A O L
B F A R M O A I I E P O R W
J N Y Y Q T R S A K S B K A
E R O H S A E O T A O B E R
T O N K M L P J P L G D R T
T E L I O C A O A W I O S C
Y S P K N G I N C T H C A Y
L D O I R B R U A C A A M A
I S R G H I E A N C R C R K
G P T R V S I A C L B L T F
F L P E P P P H C Q O E R G
N G R I R F J K A H R A U C
Q S M P H N Z F V Q M T D S
```

Solution on Page 275

BENTLEY

BEST

BIRTHDAY

BOAT

CUSTOM

DAZZLING

DISTINCT

EMERALDS

EXCLUSIVE

EXPENSIVE

FANTASY

FORTUNE

GOLD

GREATEST

HOUSE

ISLAND

JEWELRY

MANSION

MASSAGE

MEMORABLE

MONEY

PEARLS

PLATINUM

PRESENT

ROLEX

RUBIES

SAPPHIRES

SILVER

SPECIAL

SPLENDID

STUNNED

TOUR

TREASURE

TRIP

TRUCK

UNUSUAL

WEDDING

```
G E X P E N S I V E S U O H
N S T U N N E D X T R U C K
I N M U L A I C E P S G E E
D L O G N I L Z Z A D M U G
D V N I W U Y N T S E B R A
E S E Z S D S S Y R T E B S
W P Y I A N Y U A P A S T S
M L V H P A A L A T I C L A
U E N J P L D M E L N R T M
N N M R H S H S V I A A T F
I D O O I I T E T E O B F O
T I T L R N R S P B T O U R
A D S E E A I P R E S E N T
L G U X S D B E N T L E Y U
P L C J E W E L R Y N R K N
S E I B U R T R E A S U R E
```

Solution on Page 275

BARBER

BIOTIN

BLOND

BRUSH

CLEAN

CLIPS

COLOR

COMB

COSMETOLOGY

CUT

DRY

DYE

GEL

HAIR

HEALTH

HYGIENE

IRON

MOUSSE

OIL

PART

PERM

PROCESS

PRODUCT

PROTEIN

RELAXER

RIBBON

SALON

SCISSORS

SHAVE

SHINE

SHOWER

SMOOTH

SPA

STRAIGHTEN

STYLE

TOWEL

TREATMENT

TRIM

WASH

WATER

```
E C G Q D U H G K A B F I T
Q Z U R Y W H Y G I E N E H
E L Y T S Y S H O W E R T T
R R G U G U S U T T B O C H
I E O E S O E P H J O U S K
B V L N W P N G R M D U H D
B A O A S C I S S O R S A N
O H T T X A H L R B C I I O
N S E T R E S P C E B E R L
P S M T T E R C Y I T I S B
E S S U O M A D O O T A A S
R P O L W B H T R M S R W P
M E C Y E L I P M A B R A A
I S X N L N I C L E A N S P
R A U W C O L O R X N F H Q
T Z T I R O N H E A L T H V
```

Solution on Page 275

AARON	ANGELA
ABBY	ANITA
ABEL	ANNA
ABNER	ANTON
ACE	APRIL
ADELE	ARCHIBALD
ADIE	ARIEL
ADOLPH	ARLAN
ADRIAN	ARNOLD
AGATHA	ARTHUR
AHAB	ASHLEY
ALADDIN	ASHTON
ALBERT	ASPEN
ALEX	ATHENA
ALFRED	AUBREY
ALICE	AUGUST
ALLAN	AUSTIN
ALVIN	AVA
ALYSSA	
AMY	
ANASTASIA	
ANDREA	

```
O U F V R L E B A M Y R E R
J N U A E F Q T S U G U A U
J O N I D D A L A R T H U R
R R R R S N A I R D A V A B L
V A Z A S E L S R L B L R I
S A S T A L I C E B R L E R
P A N S W T H D Y E D A Y P
I L A A Y I K E A R E N B A
H F D N B L L N I T A B N N
N R O A N H A N I V L A O I
E E L G S A N L A T L H T T
P D P A A E D B E R S A H A
S X H T N E R N A G L U S K
A N E H T A E D L O N R A Q
X E L A O B A D E L E A C E
Z T Y E N C A A P N H M M W
```

Solution on Page 276

AEROBIC	RECREATION
ATHLETIC	ROAD
BREATHE	ROUTE
CARDIO	RUN
CRAMP	SHOES
DASH	SLOW
DOG	SOCKS
ENERGY	SPRINT
EXERT	STEADY
FITNESS	STRETCH
FORM	STRIDE
FRESH AIR	SWEAT
HEART	TIME
LAPS	TIRED
LEGS	TREADMILL
LEISURELY	TROT
MORNING	WARM
MUSIC	WATER
PACE	
PARK	
PATH	
POSTURE	

```
R E N E R G Y S F B D F Q R
T E R O U T E C A P A R K A
T E T R I A H S E R F L X J
O Y D A E T S E O H S L G X
R N S F W X A T L J A I N I
T W O L S L E E R E J M Q G
I R C A A H I R R I Q D D F
M C K P L S E O T C D A O R
E I S S U E B A A Q E E G C
Y T S R U I G N R K H R P R
V E E T C V N S U T X T Z A
Z L N A N R I C A R D I O M
Y H T E A I N E R U T S O P
W T I W S T R E T C H S A D
E A F S U B O P D E R I T B
C P D W A R M U S I C G E F
```

Solution on Page 276

BATH

BED

BLANKET

BRUSH

CLEAN

COVERS

COZY

CUDDLE

CURFEW

DARK

DRIFT

LATE

LIGHTS

LULLABY

MILK

MOON

MUSIC

NIGHT

NOD

PAJAMAS

PILLOW

QUIET

READ

RELAX

RESTFUL

ROUTINE

SANDMAN

SHEEP

SHOWER

SLEEP

SOFT

SOOTHE

STARS

STORY

SUNSET

TEDDY

TIRED

TUCK

WARM

YAWN

```
Z S S R E V O C Q N N Y S I
W O D T N N G D E R I T H W
N O T V H F I T Z L G J O E
N T L E C G E T L H H T W F
M H M L K R I L U F T S E R
O E E D I N E L L O A A R U
O A Q D R P A L L M R N E C
N W Z U K I H L A H L D S Z
A W M C I R F J B X U M Q M
P S A Z Q E A T Y H T A W U
X Q X Y X P T D T E S N U S
I K T D R E A D D R H U C I
P Y B F N E N D A T E B R C
C S Z A O L Y T U T E L I B
L Y R O T S S C A D P G S C
H R L E C H K L I M R A W I
```

Solution on Page 276

ADVERTISING

BRAND

BUSINESS

COLOR

COMMERCIAL

COMPANY

CONSUMER

CORPORATION

COURT

DILUTION

EMBLEM

EXCLUSIVE

IDENTIFY

IMAGE

INDICATOR

INDIVIDUAL

INFRINGEMENT

INVENTION

LAW

LOGO

MARK

NAME

ORGANIZATION

ORIGINAL

OWN

PATENT

PENDING

PHRASE

PICTURE

PRODUCT

PROPERTY

PROTECTED

REGISTER

RIGHTS

SIGN

SYMBOL

WORD

```
Y N A P M O C P I C T U R E
I R O T A C I D N I Y S C A
N N O I T U L I D T R U O C
V Y F I T N E D I O G O L J
E T O R G A N I Z A T I O N
N R L A I C R E M M O C R E
T E S L Q N L O M A R K X E
I P I A D R G A P B G C C S
O O G U E C E E W R L E S T
N R N D T W O T M U O E Y C
R P I I C O W N S E N C M U
I A D V E R T I S I N G B D
G T N I T D V A S U G T O O
H E E D O E R U N A M E L R
T N P N R H B R A N D E R P
S T I I P M L A N I G I R O
```

Solution on Page 276

BOARD

CAFE

CHEF

CHINESE

CHOICE

CHOOSE

COOK

COST

CUISINE

DESSERT

DIET

DINER

DISHES

DRINKS

EAT

FISH

FOOD

FRIES

ITEM

KIDS

LAMINATED

LIST

LUNCH

MAIN COURSE

MEXICAN

OFFERINGS

ORDER

PAPER

PHOTOS

PRICE

RESTAURANT

SALAD

SERVER

SIDES

SOUP

SPECIAL

TABLE

TIP

VARIETY

WINE

```
T X K D P Y A D E L B A T D
R S O T O H P L R C B J A T
L O O F S O U P G X I L F F
F Z C C F Q R P B O A R D E
I A C L T E A D W S E H P H
T S U E I P R I E S O O H C
E E I S E S N I T R P O E O
M D S R D E T A N I M A L S
E I I U D I U S T G T X P E
X S N O P R T R E S S E D H
I E E C A F S D I K C S C S
C C C N D I V A R I E T Y I
A A T I I S R B A I E U P D
N F N A O H G L H C N U L E
B E Q M F H C R K K R K W O
R K N T W O C R E V R E S B
```

Solution on Page 277

ABSCESS
ACCIDENT
ANEMIA
BANDAGE
BONES
CARE
CHECKUP
CLINIC
CURE
DIAGNOSIS
DOCTOR
ECZEMA
EMERGENCY
FLU
FRACTURE
GALLSTONE
HELP
HOSPITAL
HURT
INFECTION
INJURY
NEEDLE

NURSE
OFFICE
PAIN
PHARMACY
PILLS
PNEUMONIA
SCANS
SCREEN
SHOT
SPRAIN
STITCHES
SYRINGE
TEST
URGENT
VACCINE
VISIT
WEIGHT
WOUND

```
A R V I S I T B W O U N D C
H O S P I T A L Q E R U C H
S T M S T I T C H E S R E E
E C A R E A B S C E S S L C
C O R K N Y A I L I T E D K
Z D F E S T N N I S D S E U
E E M F E N D F N E F E E P
M I M C I N A E I N E N N T
A P L E H C G C C O R E I T
I N J U R Y E T S B U G A N
S I S O N G A I D M T N R E
V A C C I N E O O U C I P G
G A L L S T O N E U A R S R
T O H S L L I P C S R Y F U
P H A R M A C Y N Y F S L E
W J V H P W E I G H T R U H
```

Solution on Page 277

ARCH

BANK

BARRAGE

BARRIER

BEAVER

BLOCK

BRIDGE

BUILD

CEMENT

CONCRETE

CONTROL

DIKE

DRY

ENERGY

FLOW

GRAVITY

HEIGHT

HOOVER

IRRIGATION

LAKE

LEVEE

LOGS

NATURAL

POWER

RESERVOIR

RETAIN

RIVER

SADDLE

SAND

SPILLWAY

STEEL

STORAGE

STREAM

STRUCTURE

TIMBER

WALL

WATER

WEIR

WOOD

```
K A A A A K V V E Y X B S F W
P H R C D W S L A R U T A N D
D C O I O T E R W E I E P W
H L K O O E E G L T L E O P
B E D R V V I U L A D L O A
T P A E A E R O I I F W D V
W G L E L B R E P N E Y Q C
E P B D R T I F S R K D M S
I E D E N T G B H E I G H T
R A T O N B A Y A I R T E R
S A C E R U T C U R T S N E
W E M I R I I I B R R S E A
U E D E V C O A M A E A R M
C G V A R D N A S B L O G S
E I R L A K E O R A E V Y E
R G L L A W T H C I D R Y I
```

Solution on Page 277

ASTRO

BED

BIG

BUSINESS

CHEVY

CHILDREN

COMMERCIAL

CONVERSION

DELIVERY

DODGE

DOORS

DRIVE

DRY VAN

ECONOLINE

ENGINE

FORD

GOODS

HAUL

HONDA

LARGE

LONG

METAL

MINI

MOVING

PANEL

PASSENGER

PEOPLE

RENTAL

RIDE

SAFETY

SEATS

TOYOTA

TRANSPORT

TRAVEL

VEHICLE

VOLKSWAGEN

WHEELS

WINDOWS

WORK

```
N R E N T A L V X M R N T I
A L E D I R W H E E L S R O
V T O Y O T A T G H Q Y A E
Y O B N W N A N G O I P V L
R O L U G L E E S E O C E P
D B R K S S N R C P O D L O
D O O R S I E O D M O W S E
R D I A G W N G M L W R T P
O E P N S O A E D A I C T A
F L E Z L A R G S O N H G N
G I M I C C F T E S D W C E
I V N O I S R E V N O C H L
B E D A V O V F T R W J E T
O R L T M I N I K Y S C V N
R Y R M R G N S T A E S Y H
H O N D A H E G R A L U A H
```

Solution on Page 277

ACTIVITIES

ADVENTURE

AGING

AWARD

BENEFITS

CAKE

CAREER

CELEBRATE

COCKTAILS

COMMUNITY

DRAWING

EARLY

EASYGOING

EXERCISE

FAMILY

FISHING

FREEDOM

GARDENING

GOLFING

HOME

INCOME

LEISURE

MENTORING

PHOTOGRAPHY

PLANNING

POOLSIDE

READ

RELAX

RETIREMENT

SAILING

SAVINGS

TIME

VACATION

VOLUNTEER

WRITING

```
B N C G N I L I A S J G P Y
C G N I W A R D F E N H O L
A N S G N I V A S I O G O R
R E T I R E M E N T N N L A
E M O C N I R N O I A I S E
E O V T L U A G O V K H I X
R H U Y S L R G V I E S D E
E R A I P A Y A D T G I E R
E E E W P S C A A C N F M C
T L Q H A A E R J A I N I I
N A Y E T R B E N E F I T S
U G N I N E D R A G L M X E
L I O S L I A T K C O C A K
O N M E N T O R I N G F L A
V G C O M M U N I T Y J E C
F R E E D O M G N I T I R W
```

Solution on Page 278

BIKINI	PICNIC
BLANKET	PLAY
BOATING	RELAX
BONFIRE	REST
BUCKET	RUNNING
CASTLE	SALTY
COAST	SAND
COOLER	SHELLS
DOLPHINS	SUN
EAT	SWIM TRUNKS
FISHING	SWIMMING
FLOAT	TANNING
FRISBEE	TOWEL
FUN	TOYS
HOT	VOLLEYBALL
KIDS	WATER
LOUNGE CHAIR	WAVES
LUNCH	WIND
MUSIC	
NAPPING	
PAIL	
PARADISE	

```
P W A V E S G T O W E L N Q
L L A B Y E L L O V F S U N
U O W T A R X A L E R S F C
N R U T E W C I N C I P L N
C S K N U R T M I W S L O V
H W D K G S J S O P B A A S
Z I T I A E D N E A E Y T T
Q M T O K R C I B R E B E S
G M C S H I A H L A K I K J
G I A L Y F S P A D L K C R
N N F L T N T L N I Z I U E
I G I E L O L O K S R N B L
P A D H A B E D E E N I D O
P E N S S B O A T I N G N O
A T A N N I N G N M U S I C
N R S Y O T F G I B I M W I
```

Solution on Page 278

AIR

ALTO

BAND

BARITONE

BASS

BELL

BLOW

BLUES

BRASS

CASE

CLARINET

CLASSICAL

CLINTON

CONCERT

ENSEMBLE

GOLD

HORN

JAZZ

KENNY G

KEYS

LEARNING

MELODY

METAL

MILITARY

MOUTHPIECE

MUSIC

NOTES

ORCHESTRA

PLAY

REED

SAX

SHINY

SMOOTH

SOLO

SOPRANO

SOUND

SYMPHONY

TENOR

TONE HOLES

WIND

```
A W P T L A T E M L S W Z N
V T O N A R P O S Y V S Z F
K N H L E L O A E R Y E A F
F D R C B U T K Z A N T J B
K M N O A G L O H T O O M S
T O N E H O L E S I H N A O
C U G N I N R A E L P T U U
A T D L O G P C Y I M S X N
S H X D Y X L A H M Y A T D
E P N N N E L B M E S N E E
M I N V D P Y N I H S O N E
W E N O T I R A B B A T I R
K C L A S S I C A L R N R B
T E N O R R R R K Z U B I A A
O W L T D G V L L E B L L N
S O F A I Y P M U S I C C D
```

Solution on Page 278

ACCOUNT	OCCUPATION
ADVERTISING	OFFICE
ASSETS	PRODUCT
BILLS	PROFIT
BUILDING	PROPERTY
BUYING	PROPRIETOR
CAPITAL	PUBLIC
CAREER	RENT
CLERK	RESOURCES
CLIENT	SELLING
COMMERCE	STAFF
COMMODITY	STOCK
COMPANY	SUIT
COOPERATIVE	TRADE
EMPLOYEE	UTILITIES
ENTERPRISE	WORK
EQUITY	
FINANCIAL	
JOB	
LABOR	
LEASE	
MONEY	

```
C S L L I B Y N A P M O C F
A A E A M Y P R O P E R T Y
P L R I B O T G S N C L F N
I G H E T O N I S T R E F G
T A N Y E I R E D W E A A F
A C S I D R L V Y O M S T I
L C U L S L R I Y R M E S N
J O I J I I O T T K O M E A
O U T N O I T A P U C C O N
B N G E N T E R P R I S E C
U T R A D E I E E F O K C I
Y T C U D O R P F V R F L A
I C I L B U P O Z E D P I L
N S T O C K O O L R V A E T
G R E S O U R C E S R E N T
T E E Y O L P M E Q U I T Y
```

Solution on Page 278

BLOOM

BUDDING

BULB

BUSH

COLORFUL

CULTIVATE

DIRT

FERTILIZE

FLOURISH

FLOWER

FRUIT

GLOVES

GREEN

GROW

HARVEST

HEDGE

HERB

HOE

LEAVES

MINERALS

NOURISH

NUTRIENTS

OUTDOOR

PEAT

PLANT

POTS

RAKE

SAPLING

SEED

SKILL

SOW

SPROUT

SUNLIGHT

TALENT

TOPIARY

TREES

VITAMINS

WATER

WEED

YARD

```
D R A Y M T G F L O W E R M
J A D S U N L I G H T Z H Q
H K D E I F W P E A T I Z Z
B E M D E O X T V V I L U B
U F D O R S R I T S E I F U
L U L G O E T I I A C T T S
B Y L O E L O N V P O R A H
G R I S U U B E E L L E L S
A A K C T R S V O I O F E I
T I S D E S I T H N R H N R
I P O H E T E S N G F T T U
U O T V A R N V H A U W U O
R T O M M I N E R A L S O N
F L I X K D N W E A X P R S
G N D E E W A T E R H W P X
S T O P Q E W C J B G Z S Y
```

Solution on Page 279

BASKET

BED

BIN

BOOKS

BUCKET

CHAIR

CLOCK

COMPUTER

COOKWARE

COUCH

CUPS

CURTAIN

DISHES

FAN

FRAMES

FUTON

GLASSES

HAMPER

HANGERS

KETTLE

LAMP

LINENS

MICROWAVE

MIRROR

MOP

MUG

PANS

PHONE

PICTURES

PILLOWS

PLANT

PLUNGER

POTS

STEREO

STOVE

SWITCH

TABLE

UTENSILS

VACUUM

WASHER

Around the House

```
C B B J E I G S N R K J S K
S T O P P S N K E T T L E A
M A F M T E C P S H C U O C
I B A E N O M E R D S N B T
R L R I L A M E E C E I T N
R E L C H J V V G R M A D A
O S C H B O A B N E A T B L
R W B O T W U A A H R R U P
E O E S O C F S H S F U I C
T L S R K K P S H A K C N P
U L C E R O W L P W T E O V
P I T I S I O A U U M M T A
M P A N T S Z B R N C F U C
O H A C D Y A E C E G D F U
C P H O N E S L I S N E T U
B R X E R D M U G N I B R M
```

Solution on Page 279

BANDANA

BLANKET

BOOTS

CANDLES

CANTEEN

CHLORINE

COMPASS

FIRST AID

FLARES

FLEECE

FLINT

FOOD

GLOVES

GPS

HAT

KINDLING

KNIFE

LANTERN

LIGHTER

MAP

MEDICAL KIT

MIRROR

PONCHO

RADIO

RATIONS

ROPE

SAW

SCISSORS

SEWING KIT

SLEEPING BAG

SUNGLASSES

SUPPLIES

TAPE

TARP

TENT

TWEEZERS

TWINE

WATER

WHISTLE

WIRE

```
W A T E R P T T W I N E I L
A H E B T W E E Z E R S I F
S K F O C H L O R I N E C L
T D I O S U P P L I E S A A
H I N T I K G N I W E S N R
S A K S N R E T N A L A D E
N T B L A N K E T E D L L S
O S D C A N T E E N J G E E
I R O P E C A P A M N N S V
T I O M G G I B M I T U S O
A F F L I N T D L I A S A L
R E T H G I L D E G R W P G
A T A B T E N T P M P R M W
D T A S C I S S O R S C O I
I G U P K W H I S T L E C R
O E C E E L F P O N C H O E
```

Solution on Page 279

AUTO

BOXSTER

CAR

CLASSY

COMPANY

CONVERTIBLE

COUPE

DESIGN

DRIVING

ENGINE

EUROPEAN

EXPENSIVE

FAST

FUN

GERMAN

HYBRID

LEATHER

LOW

LUXURY

MODEL

MONEY

PANAMERA

PAYMENT

PERFORMANCE

QUALITY

RACE

RED

RICH

ROAD

SHINY

SLEEK

SMALL

SPEED

SPORTS

SPYDER

STATUS

STUTTGART

SUV

TURBO

VOLKSWAGEN

```
A S P Y D E R F G S U S D I
S P E E D Q V J H E V I S S
S P O R T S G I Y U R C U A
T O E M I C N T S B O M T P
S R T R O Y I O Y N K W A A
W E A U F L V H V F E D T N
P D P G A O I E Y A E P S A
C E Z U T U R B O S L S X M
O N Q K V T D M I T S M N E
M G H C I R U G A B D A O R
P I F B F U N T C N E L L A
A N L E D O M R S P C L S C
N E G A W S K L O V A E C E
Y B O X S T E R E H T A E L
P W O L U X U R Y E N O M T
M L O T N E M Y A P A S Q T
```

Solution on Page 279

APRIL

AUGUST

AVAILABLE

BUSY

DAY

DECEMBER

DUE

ERRAND

EVENT

FEBRUARY

GIG

INTERVIEW

JANUARY

JULY

JUNE

LOG

LUNAR

MAY

MEMOS

MONTH

NOTES

NOVEMBER

OCTOBER

PAPER

PARTY

PAY PERIOD

PLANNER

POCKET

RECORD

REMINDER

SEASON

SEPTEMBER

SESSION

TABLE

TIME

UPCOMING

VACATION

WALL

WEEK

YEAR

```
R S S U A J N W E E K Y Z H
E E E O P X D R O C E R R R
P T S A T C T E K C O P E L
A O S D S I O B U S Y D B L
P N I M O O M M G C N N O A
P O O O E I N E I I M A T W
F V N N V L R C M N G R C E
S E P T E M B E R O G R O I
N M B H N F R D P S S E J V
L B A R T A B L E Y J R U R
I E R Y U A V A I L A B L E
R R V A C A T I O N N N P Y T
P L A N N E R A U G U S T N
A W T D N U K Y T R A P N I
Z H T U U A L O G X R A E Y
G G J E C E D D D A Y M A U
```

Solution on Page 280

APPLAUD

AUDITIONS

CAPTAIN

CARTWHEEL

CHANT

CHEER

CHOREOGRAPH

CLAP

COACH

COLORS

COMPETITION

DANCE

ENCOURAGE

FLAGS

FLIP

FOOTBALL

FORMATIONS

GAME

HANDSPRING

HANDSTAND

HOLLER

JUMPS

LEAP

MOTIVATE

POPULAR

POSES

PRACTICE

PYRAMID

RALLY

ROOT

ROUTINE

SIDELINE

SPIRIT

SPOTTERS

STUNTS

TEAM

TUMBLING

UNIFORM

190

J H O L L E R O U T I N E F
U C C O L O R S R E E H C L
M A H A N D S P R I N G I A
P O E P P O P U L A R F T G
S C D N A T S D N A H O C S
M L S S I R A L L Y O O A A
R E S R N L G I Q R M T R P
O E T P E O E O N P S B P P
F H N A I T I D E I E A T L
I W U E V R T T I R S L N A
N T T L F I I O A S O L A U
U R S W L T T T P M P H H D
T A U D I T I O N S R A C A
E C C O P Y R A M I D O L N
A E N C O U R A G E N E F C
M T U M B L I N G A M E G E

Solution on Page 280

BEAK

BILL

CHICKS

CUCKOO

DOVE

DUCK

EAGLE

EGG

EXTINCTION

FALCON

FEATHER

FINCH

FLY

FOOD

GOOSE

HAWK

HUMMINGBIRD

MIGRATE

NEST

ORNITHOLOGY

OSTRICH

OWL

PARROT

PECK

PENGUIN

PERCH

PIGEON

PLUMAGE

PREY

ROBIN

SEEDS

SING

SOAR

SONG

SWAN

TAIL

TREE

TURKEY

VERTEBRATE

WING

```
O M A N A W S Y C K O B O Y
Y F C T O S I E T S E N M E
U A U U H K T F E A T H E R
T L C K Y C E U K D U T T P
S C K Z Z I I K R M S A A I
D O O F N H N R M K L I R Y
K N O I T C N I T X E L G H
F C I A W I N G U S Y Y I K
P L U M A G E H V G O Z M B
X U Y D B S T N F I N C H O
O R N I T H O L O G Y E X I
V E R T E B R A T E A Z P G
W D S O S D R K R G G E N N
V O T O B A A C L V R I R O
K V L W O I P E J C S H P S
E E R T H G N P H A W K X M
```

Solution on Page 280

AKC

BACK

BARK

BLACK

BROWN

CANINE

CHASE

COLOR

COMPANION

CUTE

DOG

EARS

EXERCISE

FUR

HOUND

HUNT

KENNEL

LEASH

LEGS

LONG

LOYAL

MINI

MUSCULAR

PAWS

PET

PIEBALD

PUPPY

RABBIT

RACE

SCENT

SHORT

SIT

SMALL

SNOUT

STUBBY

TAN

TRAIN

WALK

WHITE

WIENER

Solution on Page

```
W S U H F B E S N K D E E C
S H C L S S R R T L H W A M
A O I E I A A O A K C N R M
A R Z T N C E B W V I J S W
D T U W E T E L E N N E K L
U E M E S I C R E X E C C T
S W T M P B O A B S A S A V
G T A U H B M L D L A N B K
E L P L C A P U B H M H R H
L P D D K R A C B O F A C U
Y C G N E O N S T U B B Y N
T U O N S L I U R N I A R T
F E E W O O O M Q D N M E Z
L I A Y N C N M I G O P L L
W P A U S S Q W X N V H P R
S L O N G O D W T I I I P E
```

Solution on Page 280

ACTIVISM

AMERICAN

BERNARD

BROOKLYN

BUDGET

BURLINGTON

CANDIDATE

CARPENTER

CAUCUSING

CHAIR

COMMITTEE

CONGRESS

DEBATES

DEMOCRAT

FILIBUSTER

FILMMAKER

LEFT

MAYOR

NEW YORK

ORGANIZER

OUTSPOKEN

POLICIES

PROFESSOR

PROMINENCE

REFORM

REPUTATION

RESEARCHER

SOCIALISM

VOICE

VOTE

WRITER

```
K C H A I R O S S E F O R P
D M A Y O R G A N I Z E R X
E N A C I R E M A R K F X V
B R O O K L Y N E A I S S J
A Y N M D P Q F M L H Z O R
T E O M P R O M I N E N C E
E M T I Z R L B G O T E I H
S S G T M I U N S I A K A C
S I N T F S I T E T D O L R
E V I E T S E A I A I P I A
R I L E U G L R C T D S S E
G T R C D V E C I U N T M S
N C U U O T F O L P A U V E
O A B I I E T M O E C O O R
C N C R E T N E P R A C T V
N E W Y O R K D R A N R E B
```

Solution on Page 281

ART

BAMBOO

BIGHT

BLANKET

CABLE

COLOR

COUNT

CRAFT

DESIGN

FABRIC

GAUGE

HAT

HOBBY

HOOK

KNIT

LACE

LENGTH

LONG

LOOP

MATERIALS

METAL

PAIR

PATTERN

PIN

POINT

ROD

SETS

SEWING

SINGLE

SIZE

SOCKS

STITCH

STRAIGHT

TAPER

TECHNIQUES

THIN

TOOL

WEAVE

WOOD

WORK

```
L B G B U C X W H L L S D H
N I P N V S L O O P O E O J
I A M E O T N U O C O L O R
H K Z Q B L A N K E T G W T
T I N K X P A T T E R N N H
S A Y G P N S K C O S I Y U
U U P M S G G H K I O S M Z
K U U E E B N I C P R Y E D
M A T E R I A L S T C B T H
K S F I Q S L M M E I A A H
Y F A U I E E A B W D T L F
P P E K C W N S C O E F S V
U S T R A I G H T E O A G P
H R T O B N T H G I B R V Z
A X V W L G H O B B Y C O E
T W T O E G U A G I Y R E D
```

Solution on Page 281

APRON

BASTE

BEAT

BLEND

BOWL

BREAD

BROWN

CAKE

CASSEROLE

COOL

CREAM

CRUST

CUP

EGGS

FLOUR

GLAZE

GOURMET

HEAT

INGREDIENTS

KNEAD

MIX

OVEN

PAN

POWDER

RACK

RECIPE

RISE

ROLLER

SALT

SEASONED

SHAPE

SODA

SPOON

STIR

SUGAR

TEMPERATURE

TIMER

WATER

WHIP

YEAST

200

```
F B J H Y W B O W L P P H Y
M E E N E J R D R A A T L H
F A R F A O V E N I T A R H
T S P U S V L N D M A E R C
Y C M R T L Z O C W P B R O
Z A N J O A D S B I O I U O
L S S R T N R A C K D P H L
F S T N E I D E R G N I I W
C E T L M K R S P M A B T N
S R B S R C N N H M P A I W
T O G N U U F E Y J E S M O
E L D P O R O G A E K T E R
J E A A G A C L P D A E R B
E M I S G G E A F J C S M Z
T L P L Y U H Z J S T I R V
B N O O P S F E J Y X R S Z
```

Solution on Page 281

BARTER

BUY

CAPITAL

COMMODITY

COMPETE

CONSUMER

CORPORATE

DEMAND

DOLLAR

ECONOMY

EXCHANGE

FINANCE

FORCES

GOODS

GOVERNMENT

INFLATION

INNOVATION

INVESTMENT

LABOR

LAWS

MARKET

MONEY

NEED

OWNERSHIP

PRICE

PRODUCER

PROFIT

REGULATIONS

RESOURCES

SELL

SERVICES

STOCK

TAKEOVER

TRADE

TREASURY

VALUE

WAGE

```
E D A R T E K R A M W A G E L
L T R E A S U R Y E C I R P
D O L L A R E T R A B Y U R
L E S J S P I H S R E N W O
A E E N D D E M A N D B N D
T T Q N O A N L O W E G S U
I A Y M O I C M S G S O E C
P R M N G I T O N E S V C E
A O O S O G T A N E C E R R
C P N B E I H A L S M R U T
O R O U A C T L V U U N O I
M O C Y X L I A K O G M S F
P C E E U L A V L C N E E O
E T A K E O V E R F O N R R
T S I N V E S T M E N T I P
E C N A N I F L A W S I S C
```

Solution on Page 281

ACOUSTIC

AMPLIFIER

APPLAUSE

AUDIENCE

BAND CAMP

BASS

BATON

BRASS

CLARINET

CONDUCTOR

COUNTRY

DRUMS

ELECTRIC

ENCORE

FAMOUS

FANS

FIDDLE

GIG

GROUPIES

GUITAR

HARMONICA

KEYBOARD

MARCH

PARADE

POP

PRACTICE

ROADIES

ROCK

SAXOPHONE

SINGER

SOLO

SPEAKERS

STAGE

STRINGS

TROMBONE

TRUMPET

TUBA

VOCALIST

XYLOPHONE

```
G I G C I R T C E L E S O F
V E C I T C A R P R N L R I
T D C I T S U O C A O K E D
S R A T I U G T F S H C G D
R A U B A N D C A M P O N L
E O X M A D R U M S O R I E
K B A O P S N D P E L G S D
A Y V C P E S N L C Y R C A
E E O O I H T O I N X O L R
P K C U S N O C F E T U A A
S N A N E H O N I I U P R P
S O L T I C P M E D B I I E
A T I R D R O V R U A E N G
R A S Y A A P P L A U S E A
B B T R O M B O N E H B T T
S G N I R T S U O M A F N S
```

AMPHIBIAN

AREAS

BENEFIT

BIRDLIFE

BOREAL

COASTAL

DIVERSITY

ECOLOGY

ENHANCE

FAUNA

FEATURES

FISH

FOREST

HABITATS

HUMANITY

LANDSCAPE

LAWS

MAMMALS

MANAGED

MARINE

MIGRATORY

NATIONAL

NATURAL

NEST

OWLS

PLANTS

PRESERVE

PRIVATE

REFUGE

REPTILE

RESEARCH

RESOURCES

SPECIAL

THREATS

TREES

TUNDRA

WEB

WILDLIFE

```
B E N E F I T A R E A S Z S
S Y R G P R I V A T E P B T
T R F U M A R I N E W E I A
N O O F O S C A B T V C R E
A T R E Y T I S R E V I D R
L A E R O B T E D S W A L H
P R S M I A E C H N L L I T
E G T H T S E R U T A E F U
C I P I O C L U M W N L E N
N M B R D O I O A I O A C D
A A R D E A T S N L I R O R
H K K E G S P E I D T U L A
N E S T A T E R T L A T O F
E F A U N A R R Y I N A G I
M A M M A L S Z V F I N Y S
S L W O M H R E S E A R C H
```

Solution on Page 282

AMERICA

AREA

BEACH

BEEF

BOLIVIA

BRAZIL

BUENOS AIRES

CLIMATE

COUNTRY

CULTURE

EMPANADAS

EVITA

FEDERATION

GAUCHO

GEOGRAPHY

HISTORY

LAND

LATIN

LITERATURE

MOUNTAINS

MUSIC

NATURE

PAMPAS

PARAGUAY

PATAGONIA

PESO

PLAINS

POLITICS

PROVINCE

REPUBLIC

SILVER

SOCCER

SPAIN

SUBTROPICAL

TANGO

TOURIST

TRAVEL

WINE

```
O N N A T U R E P U B L I C
S I L V E R U T L U C E R S
E A C L I M A T E S C E A N
P P L D N A L N A N C D I I
B S U B T R O P I C A L N A
E X A S R S M V O N H I O L
A F N N A A O S A S T T G P
C E T I P R Z P C A R E A A
H D R A P W M I L U O R T T
I E A T I E T C L G A A A I
S R V N R I I O R G M T P V
T A E U L S H A U M E U O E
O T L O U C P A F R R R G F
R I P M U H Y J Q O I E N E
Y O F A Y R T N U O C S A E
H N G Q B O L I V I A W T B
```

Solution on Page 282

BEADS

BRASS

CHROME

COIN

COPPER

CROWN

DIME

DISCO BALL

DISHES

EMERALD

FOIL

GEMS

GLASS

GLITTER

GLOSS

GOLD

HAIR

JEWELRY

LIGHTS

MARBLES

MEDAL

METAL

MIRROR

NICKEL

PEARLS

PENNY

PLATINUM

QUARTZ

REFLECTION

RUBY

SILVER

SPOON

STAR

STEEL

SUN

TIARA

TINSEL

TROPHY

WATER

WINDOWS

```
N I O C R L E E T S S O L G
O L E I U N A I D W D M G D
O W A F B U N S I O M A E X
P H D D Y S L E S D J T E G
S I L V E R P H C N E I O B
C R O L A M L S O I W A Y Q
M O G E J F A I B W E R M M
V R P I Z U T D A S L A W J
O R L P R C I D L A R E M E
Y I I G E H N R L B Y M W V
H M O L T R U N L X Z I E Y
P M F I A O M E I N X D V N
O E R T W M S Y G C R O W N
R T H T V E X G H N K A A E
T A G E Q U A R T Z G E T P
V L H R G L A S S A R B L S
```

Solution on Page 282

APPLES

BEER

CAKE

CARROTS

CELERY

CHEESE

CREAM

DAIRY

DRESSING

EGGS

FRUIT

JAM

JELLY

JUICE

KETCHUP

LEFTOVERS

LEMONADE

LETTUCE

LIGHT BULB

MARGARINE

MEAT

MILK

MUSHROOMS

MUSTARD

OLIVES

ONION

ORANGES

PEPPERS

PICKLES

PLUM

RELISH

ROLLS

SALSA

SAUCE

SHELVES

SODA

SYRUP

TEA

TOMATOES

YOGURT

Refrigerator Contents

```
S L J E L L Y J Z M A E R C
H S E E K A C T R U G O Y N
E T H F E C I U J S F N R P
L I G H T B U L B H W I I E
V U M O C O W D E R K O A P
E R A B H Y V R N O J N D P
S F A E U D N E I O G P S E
L I D E P R D S R M M L C R
S T O R R A C S A S L U L S
P C S M N T M I G O A M E E
I E I O R S E N R S Y G C S
C L M T P U A G A Q N U H A
K E A U I M T O M A T O E S
L R R H S I L E R T Z T E M
E Y S E V I L O E S A L S A
S V K O A P P L E S G G E J
```

Solution on Page 283

AARDVARK

ANIMALS

BABOON

BIRDS

BUFFALO

CHEETAH

CONTINENT

CROCODILE

DESERT

DRY

ELEPHANT

FISH

GAZELLE

GIRAFFE

GORILLA

GRASS

HEDGEHOG

HIPPO

HYENA

IMPALA

INSECTS

ISLANDS

LEMUR

LION

MAMMALS

MONKEY

NATURE

OSTRICH

PARK

PLAINS

PYTHON

REPTILES

RHINO

RIVER

SEAS

SNAKE

TROPICS

WARTHOG

WILDLIFE

ZEBRA

```
M Z M B E L S P P P S D R I B
A E G A U F I N J Y X G I L
M B A L B F I O A T T O T N
M R Z A G K F L N K N H R G
A A E P Q R H A D W E T O T
L N L M A A H A L L N R P N
S E L I T P E R I O I A I C
T Y E E E R S D K L T W C H
S H E L U G O V L Y N W S I
T H E T E C I A S H O H N P
C R A D O M N R S S C M I P
E N E R G I U K A I G O A O
S Z C S M E N R R F C N L N
N F S A E S H T G X F K P I
I S L A N D S O R I V E R H
B S B A B O O N G D R Y H R
```

Solution on Page 283

ACOUSTIC

AMPLIFY

BAND

BASS

BLUES

BRIDGE

CHORD

COUNTRY

ELECTRIC

FINGERS

FLAMENCO

FRET

GIG

HEAD

HEEL

INLAY

JACK

LINING

MELODY

MODULATE

MUSIC

NECK

NOTE

NUT

OCTAVE

PEG

PICK

PITCH

PLUG

RELIEF

RHYTHM

RIFF

ROCK

ROOT

SADDLE

STAND

STRAP

TEMPO

TONE

TUNE

Solution on Page

Puzzles

Play Guitar

```
Z G U L P V U C E V A T C O
K R C F I D R O H C O M A L
I G R L T Y X T O E H J I A
K I Q A C I S U M T A N N X
P C A M H F S N Y C I D L A
J H E E C T F H K N E Y A M
F E G N I S R E G N I F Y J
P E P C R I E F E F F I R T
P L I O T K T N B Q C L O A
F D Q L C T U K L O A P C U
R D Y I E T A L U D O M K B
K A P M L R G N E P B A A V
R S P V E U T I S T A N D R
K O Z T B R I D G E D R A C
E N O T Y D O L E M B A T F
I N S T I M J A Q C B A S S
```

ALARM

ALERT

BIRD

BLOW

BREEZE

CALL

COACH

COMMUNICATION

COMPETITION

CUE

FINGERS

FLUTE

HARMONY

JOY

KIDS

LIPS

LOUD

MELODY

MOUTH

MUSIC

NOISE

NOTES

PITCH

POLICE

PRACTICE

PUCKER

SHARP

SIGNAL

SONG

SOUND

SPORTS

START

STOP

TAXI

TEETH

TONGUE

TOOT

TRAIN

TUNE

WIND

```
E D Q G O G Z E R O J T C Q
Z V N Y Z F I E C I L O P T
H O N D P Z K I D S M N Y D
S T R O P S S W N M Q G C A
O I E L I U Y I U L O U D E
U H C E M T U N E L S E S T
N S Z M T N I D O P H T M U
D T C O A C H T U M A I O L
S O G E A T A C E R R X U F
C P U T Z R K L T P P A T I
E S I O N E T E L I M T H N
L O E L R L E R U R P O X G
N U G T T A P R A C T I C E
F E B L O W B L B I R D E R
V O V X O N A J L A N G I S
J A K Q T F Y D B U W D U P
```

Solution on Page 283

ALARM

BAT

BED

BLANKET

CAMPFIRE

CANDLES

CLUB

CRICKETS

DANCING

DARK

DINNER

DREAMS

FIREFLIES

FIREWORKS

GHOST

INSOMNIA

MIDNIGHT

MONSTERS

MOON

MOVIES

NIGHTMARE

NOCTURNAL

NOVEL

OWL

PAJAMAS

PARTY

PLANETS

PREDATORS

QUIET

RACCOONS

REST

SLEEP

SLIPPERS

SNORING

STAR

STORY

SUNSET

TOOTHBRUSH

VAMPIRE

WEREWOLF

```
C Z P N A B U L C P E E L S
A U L O L D D A R K T E K S
N G A V A A I A I T S R Y U
D N N E R N C G C O O A T N
L I E L M C O R K W H M R S
E R T O O I S C E L G T A E
S O S O S N E R T N Z H P T
L N N Y T G I T S U N G R E
I S P D A F L T S E R I E K
P E A E R I F P M A C N D N
P I J W E R E W O L F O A A
E V A H S U R B H T O O T L
R O M I D N I G H T B M O B
S M A E R D F V A M P I R E
X H S Y X M O N S T E R S D
S T O R Y V Q U I E T A B E
```

Solution on Page 284

AEROBICS

BAT

BOAT

BOXING

CAMPING

CATCH

COACH

DANCE

EXTREME

FIELD

FISH

GOAL

GOLF

GYMNASTICS

HIKING

HOCKEY

HOME RUN

KARATE

LACROSSE

LEAGUE

MARATHON

NET

OLYMPICS

PLAYER

RACING

RALLY

REFEREE

RUGBY

RUNNING

SKI

SNOWSHOE

SOCCER

STADIUM

SUPER BOWL

TEAM

TENNIS

TRACK

WIN

WRESTLE

YACHT

```
E F I S H C A O C S S Q H Y
K T E N N I S A M N O Y C O
G C G U H Y M A G O C E T L
N Y A N G P R E S W C K A Y
I L M R I A R I O S E C C M
X L V N T C E E H H R O T P
O A G H A A A L F O F H P I
B R O S O S B R S E C X L C
W N Z C B M T S W A R T A S
H I K I N G E I Y I C E Y L
R U G B Y H N R C K W N E A
T L W O B R E P U S M C R O
E M E R T X E R U N N I N G
A W R E S T L E T A R A K O
M S T A D I U M D L E I F L
A Y U V Y Z B U S R F H L F
```

Solution on Page 284

AFTERNOON

APPLE

BAGEL

BANANA

BROWNIES

CAKE

CANDY

CARROTS

CELERY

CEREAL

CHEESE

CHIPS

CHOCOLATE

COOKIES

CROISSANT

DAILY

DIP

FRUIT

FUDGE

GRANOLA

HEALTHY

JERKY

KIDS

MORNING

MUSHROOMS

NACHOS

NUTS

OLIVES

ORANGE

PICKLES

POPCORN

RAISINS

ROLLS

SCONE

SEEDS

SPICY

SPREADS

TASTY

TOAST

TREAT

Solution on Page

```
W S L L O R A N G E L P P A
S E V I L O V N R I S I N V
P S E L K C I P A N A N A B
R F I Y D N A C N D S L C F
E A J E R K Y Y O W E V H R
A Y I O N H N Y L T I B O U
D C M S T O R R A C K R S I
S E H L I E C L F S O O E T
J R A I L N O S T P O W G S
U E W E P C S U E O C N D A
H A C J O S N R R P Q I U O
S L C H E E S E N C K E F T
E E C M U S H R O O M S Q R
E G T N A S S I O R C A K E
D A I L Y J V M N N P I D A
S B M S P I C Y T S A T O T
```

Solution on Page 284

ACRES

ANIMALS

BARN

CATTLE

CHICKENS

COMBINE

CORN

COUNTRY

COWS

CROPS

CULTIVATE

DAIRY

DUCKS

EGGS

FAMILY

FEED

FIELDS

FOOD

FRUIT

GARDEN

GOATS

GRAINS

GROW

HARVEST

HORSES

HOUSE

LAND

LIVESTOCK

MILKING

PIG

PLANTATION

PRODUCE

RANCH

SHEEP

SILO

STABLE

TRACTOR

VEGETABLES

WAGON

WHEAT

```
Y H N Q C G A R D E N E N W
B L O H C N A R Z H N S S H
W X I U I W F R U I T I C E
H H T M S B P O B A L Y R A
O S A C A E A M O O I R O T
R L T R F F O G Z D V T P O
S F N A I C H I C K E N S D
E E A E B B A C R E S U B J
S E L V I L T R A C T O R H
Q D P B P E E H S W O C Y N
S N E T A V I T L U C E R S
K O G I P T O G N I K L I M
C G G Y T S E V R A H T A T
U A S N I A R G R O W T D O
D W P R O D U C E F L A N D
S K D C O R N O R V G C B O
```

Solution on Page 284

ART

BASKET

BRACELET

BROACH

CLAY

COIL

CORD

CRAFT

CREATE

CRIMP

CUTTER

DESIGN

FANCY

FINDINGS

FUN

GIFT

GLASS

HOBBY

HOLE

JEWELRY

JIG

KNOT

LOOM

MAKE

NECKLACE

NEEDLE

PATTERN

PLIERS

PONY

PURSE

REAMER

SEED

SELL

SEWING

THREAD

TIE

TRAY

TRIM

WIRE

WOOD

```
Z J H B A S K E T S T A C R
H N V R S R E I L P S R E D
M O E A W X P L N M A A I R
A X L C Y S E E D F M B L M
N T I E K C U T T E R O A G
Y P D L F L G R R O E J O N
L O A E U I A I A J E N C L
L N A T S P N C F W W O O D
B Y W H T I H D E T A E R C
P M I R C E G L I O K F D M
G A R E D C R N G N I W E S
H K E A R Y B N U K G F S E
T E C D C B H R X F I S R L
Z R L N D B T H L V J U U L
E Q A L I O C E L N P L P I
M F Y Y M H Q P A K M L W Z
```

Solution on Page 285

ASSIST

BLOSSOMS

BUSINESS

CLASSES

CONSISTS

CROSSES

DISCUSS

DRESSES

FOSSILS

GLASSES

GRASSES

GUESSES

ISSUES

KISSES

LESSONS

LOSSES

MASSES

MESSES

PASSES

POSSESS

PRESSES

RESTLESS

SADNESS

SAUSAGES

SEASONS

SEESAWS

SENSES

SESSION

SICKNESS

SISTERS

SPLASHES

STRESS

SUCCESS

SUGGESTS

SUSPENSE

SWISS

SYSTEMS

USELESS

VESSELS

```
S E S S E R P S Y S T E M S
O S E U F S I S T E R S T M
S A E K G O S L O S S E S D
E D S S S G S E S S E U G I
I S N A T S D E S E A S O N S
S E W S E R R S I P P R E C
I S S I N E T E T L E S U U
O S E S K S S V Z S S I W S
N E U N C S L A T A S R S S
M S S O I E S L L U E P U E
A S S C S S E C N S L K S S
S E I S I S U N D A E I P S
S M O S S O L B S G S S E A
E N T Y R P X H Q E U S N L
S C R O S S E S E S E S N E S G
S U C C E S S G R A S S E S
```

ACTIVITIES

ANIME

ART

ATTENDEES

AUTOGRAPHS

BOOK

CITIES

COLLECTIBLE

COMIC

CONVENTION

COSPLAY

CREATORS

CULTURE

DISTRIBUTORS

ENTHUSIASTS

EVENT

FANS

ILLUSTRATIONS

INDUSTRY

MANGA

NEW YORK

PASSES

PRESENTATIONS

PROFIT

PUBLISHERS

RETAILERS

SHOWS

TOYS

VENUES

VIDEO GAME

VOLUNTEERS

WEEKEND

```
K O A Y A L P S O C I M O C
O K H Z E C I N D U S T R Y
O H C R E A T O R S H O W S
B P D I S T R I B U T O R S
V E P R O F I T V E N U E S
I L L U S T R A T I O N S S
D B P C N S U T I K T G L R
E I A U A H T N E V E I S E
O T S L F P S E I T I C E H
G C S T S A I S U H T N E S
A E E U Y R W E E K E N D I
M L S R O G K R O Y W E N L
E L Q E T O A P A N I M E B
P O N O I T N E V N O C T U
Z C V O L U N T E E R S T P
S R E L I A T E R A G N A M
```

Solution on Page 285

ANGLE

APERTURE

ART

BATTERY

BLUR

BODY

BUTTONS

CANVAS

CENTER

COPY

DEVELOP

DIGITAL

DISTANCE

FILM

FLASH

FOCUS

FRAME

GAMMA

HOOD

ILLUSTRATION

IMAGE

LENS

LIGHT

MEGAPIXELS

NEGATIVE

PERSPECTIVE

PHOTOGRAPHS

PICTURE

POSE

SECURITY

SETTING

SHOTS

SHUTTER

STUDIO

SUBJECT

TIMER

TRIPOD

VIDEO

VIEWS

ZOOM

Solution on Page

```
Y P O C P U U S W E I V L M
N H S A L F O C U S Y I S O
O O P O L E V E D B G D T O
I T R C A N V A S H H E O Z
T O S E C U R I T Y O O H B
A G U E T O B U T T O N S R
R R B M S N S D Y A D L E E
T A J A A L E R Y T G S L T
S P E R S P E C T I V E G T
U H C F D T E X T M L T N U
L S T B T R I R I A L T A H
L T L A U A I M T P S I S S
I U B T Q P M I E U A N F T
R D C I O G G M F R R G E X
O I J D D I S T A N C E E L
P O R W D P O S E G A M I M
```

Solution on Page 285

ACTIVE

ANIMAL

ATTIC

BARN

BLIND

BROWN

BURROW

CAT

CHEESE

COMPUTER

DARK

DISNEY

EAT

FIELD

HERBIVORE

HOLE

HOUSE

HUNT

JERRY

KITCHEN

MAMMAL

MICKEY

MINNIE

NEST

NOCTURNAL

NOSE

PET

PLAYFUL

PREY

QUIET

RODENT

RUN

SMALL

SNOUT

TAIL

TIMID

TRAP

VERMIN

WHITE

WILD

```
N H C L T S E N B X Z D C C
N O S E I W T O A C W V S I
V L J P M A O C R O D E N T
H E E S I I T R N M A L O T
H S R X D F N P R P R N U A
I U R M D L L N W U K E T D
N O Y Y I A A Y I T B H W P
Q H K W Y N M E L E E C E S
E P T F L R I K D R V T M J
C D U T L U N C B X I I Q E
X L D E A T A I R Z T K C J
D E P I M C V M S F C B V B
E I T U S O M A M M A L G H
K F A Q R N W O R B T I U L
C H E E S E E T I H W N T E
B T R A P R E Y X K T D I F
```

Solution on Page 286

ANIMALS

ART

BALL

BATS

BIKE

BLOCKS

BOOKS

BOXES

BUS

CHESS

COMPUTER

COWBOY HAT

CRAFTS

CRAYONS

DIRT

DOLL

FIGURES

GAMES

INSTRUMENTS

JUNGLE GYM

LEGOS

MUSIC

PAN

PLANE

PUPPET

PUZZLE

REMOTE

RUBBER DUCK

SHOVEL

SLIDE

SPOON

STICK HORSE

STICKERS

SWINGS

TEA SET

TOY

TRAIN

TRIKE

TRUCKS

WAGON

Solution on Page

```
G B W W B O X E S S E H C T
I E N A L P Q J G W W B J R
T N N T G E S L A M I N A U
O E S O A O G R M K S N H C
Y S P T O H N O E N T L G K
B E T P R P Y A S K I R Z S
S M Z A U U S O P J C A I Z
H B Y Z B P M Y B V K I R D
O A Z G B M S E C W H S T T
V L X O E E E O N Q O K E S
E L O K R L M D C T R C S N
L K I U D P G Q I M S O A O
S R G L U O X N S L E L E Y
T I C T C A L B U S S B T A
F W E X K R W L M J Y W W R
J R E M O T E L S T F A R C
```

Solution on Page 286

ADVISORY

AUTHORITY

BANKS

BEIGE BOOK

BOARD

BUSINESS

CONDITIONS

CONGRESS

CONSUMER

CRISIS

DECISIONS

DEPOSITS

DIVIDEND

ECONOMY

EMPLOYMENT

FINANCIAL

FOMC

GOVERNORS

INDICATOR

LIQUIDITY

OVERSEEING

POLICY

PRICES

RATES

REGULATION

REPORT

RESEARCH

STABILIZING

SUPERVISING

SYSTEM

VOTE

```
S D N E D I V I D R A O B S
D S S R O N R E V O G T B I
R E H H B G B U S I N E S S
E D C O V E R S E E I N G I
P S R I A Y U G M G Z A R R
O N A L S C Q Y E R I U E C
R O E E N I O B T A L T M F
T I S F T L O R S T I H U I
C T E O P O P N Y E B O S N
O I R M K P V P S S A R N A
N D E C R E G U L A T I O N
G N I S I V R E P U S T C C
R O T A C I D N I F I Y E I
E C O N O M Y R O S I V D A
S K N A B Y T I D I U Q I L
S T I S O P E D S E C I R P
```

Solution on Page 286

BANANA

BROWNIE

BUBBLEGUM

BUTTERSCOTCH

CAKE

CARAMEL

CHERRY

CHOCOLATE

COBBLER

COFFEE

CONE

COOKIE

COTTON CANDY

FLOAT

FRUIT

GREEN TEA

HARD

JUBILEE

LEMON

MANGO

MAPLE WALNUT

MOCHA

ORANGE

OREO

PEACH

PECAN

PISTACHIO

PRALINES

RAINBOW

RASPBERRY

RIPPLE

ROCKY ROAD

SANDWICH

SAUCE

SOFT

SUNDAE

TOPPINGS

VANILLA

```
E B M D Z M E E L I B U J U
I D U P R A S P B E R R Y T
K R G T L P I S T A C H I O
O A E W T L E M A R A C Y P
O H L O C E C U A S J D T P
C R B B H W R H B N N F I I
M I B N O A L S E A G Q U N
V P U I C L E P C R N O R G
A P B A O N M N E O R A F S
N L K R L U O E E C T Y N E
I E P F A T N R C K A C A A
L G E L T T O O I Y T N H D
L N A O E I N W O R B F C N
A A C A R E L B B O C B O U
U R H T S E N I L A R P M S
C O F F E E S A N D W I C H
```

Solution on Page 286

BAG

BEAR

BLANKET

BURGERS

CABIN

CAMPER

CANOE

CLIMBING

COMPASS

COOKING

COOLER

DRINKS

EXPLORING

FAMILY

FIRE

FISH

FOOD

FOREST

FRIENDS

GUIDEBOOK

HIKE

INSECT

LAKE

LANTERN

MAPS

NATURE

OUTDOORS

PARK

POND

RANGER

ROAST

SNACKS

STARS

STORIES

SUNSCREEN

SWIMMING

TACKLE

TENT

TRAIL

WILDLIFE

```
S T I H Z S E I R O T S J K
Y T E N G D J T S J X G G R
V L A N S N F I S H J N A A
E P I R T E I S A E I I B P
R S S M S I C M P B R K N E
E Q U N A R F T M L F O Y L
P X I N A F O I O I M O F K
M A P S S C L O C A W C B C
A S N L W C K A D R Q S L A
C K R A O I R S K T U U A T
N N E E T R L E C E U E N S
G I T K G U I D E B O O K A
F R N F I R R N L N R N E O
I D A O N H U E G I R A T R
R E L O O C A B I N F C E S
E B A D N O P R A N G E R B
```

Solution on Page 287

BAKING

BALLOONS

BAND

BARTENDER

BIRTHDAY

CAKE

CATERER

CLEANING

COOKING

DATE

DELEGATE

DESIGN

DESSERT

DINNER

DRINKS

EVENT

FAVORS

FLOWERS

FOOD

GAMES

GIFTS

GRADUATION

GUESTS

HIRE

INVITATIONS

LINEN

LOCATION

MANAGER

MEAL

MENU

MUSIC

ORGANIZE

PROMOTE

PUBLICITY

ROOM

SCHEDULE

SEATING

SNACKS

TABLE

THEME

```
S T S E U G O R G A N I Z E
G N I N A E L C E V E N T Y
N D O O F M S T F I G A T R
I F L O W E R S E N G I E E
K I G F L A G E I E C D L G
O E N A P L R K L I N B A A
O T I V B H A E L E A M N N
C O T O I B D B T T E O T A
I M A R R T U R W S I D R M
S O E S T P A C A T E R E R
U R S N H B T T A S O N S E
M P K A D V I C I O U L S M
C O N C A A O G M O I I E E
A B I K Y L N R E N N I D H
K T R S E L U D E H C S F T
E T D E T A D N A B T V R E
```

Solution on Page 287

ATLANTIC COAST

BANKING

BEACHES

BELLEFONTE

BLADES

CAMDEN

CHESWOLD

CLAYTON

COLONIAL

DOVER

ELSMERE

FENWICK ISLAND

FORT CHRISTINA

HARRINGTON

KENT

LENAPE

MIDDLETOWN

MILLSBORO

NANTICOKE

NEW CASTLE

OCEAN VIEW

RESORTS

RIVERFEST

SELBYVILLE

SUSSEX

THE WEDGE

TOWNSEND

WILMINGTON

WOODLAND FERRY

```
K B S T R O S E R H R V G E
E E G H N E D M A C E C N L
N A E E B L O R J M V O I S
T C K W F L R I M A O L K M
W H O E E I O V I N D O N E
I E C D N V B E D I O N A R
L S I G W Y S R D T C I B E
M W T E I B L F L S E A D N
I O N P C L L E E I A L N O
N L A A K E I S T R N B E T
G D N N I S M T O H V L S Y
T E X E S S U S W C I A N A
O B E L L E F O N T E D W L
N E W C A S T L E R W E O C
A T L A N T I C C O A S T L
E W O O D L A N D F E R R Y
```

Solution on Page 287

ALBUM

ALTERNATIVE

ATLANTIC

AWARDS

BAND

BERRYMAN

BRIAN ENO

BRITISH

BUCKLAND

CAPITOL

CHAMPION

CLOCKS

DRUMMER

ELECTRONIC

FIX YOU

GRAMMY

GUITAR

INK

MAGIC

MIDNIGHT

PARACHUTES

PARADISE

PARLOPHONE

PHIL HARVEY

PIANO

POPULAR

ROCK

SAFETY

SHIVER

SONG

STUDIO

TOURS

TROUBLE

TRUE LOVE

WHAT IF

WORLDWIDE

YELLOW

```
D U R A T I U G S H I V E R
A W A R D S Z H S I T I R B
T Y B A N D N A M Y R R E B
L E D I W D L R O W U L S A
A L N P S B R I A N E N O L
N L P O I D U T S C L P N B
T O T A H A S D T C O W G U
I W M E R P N R L P V H M M
C R A W R A O O U K E A I L
T E G O L N C L I O N T D O
R M I K I K A H R P T I N T
O M C C S R C T U A M F I I
U U O Y X I F O I T P A G P
B R P H I L H A R V E Y H A
L D H P A R A D I S E S T C
E B S A F E T Y M M A R G V
```

Solution on Page 287

ALLOY

APPLIANCES

AUTOMOBILES

BAR

BEAM

BRIDGE

BUILD

CAR

CUTLERY

GRADE

HARD

HEAVY

INDUSTRY

KNIVES

LOCKS

MANGANESE

MANUFACTURING

MELT

METAL

MILL

MINING

NAIL

ORE

PITTSBURGH

PLATE

RECYCLING

ROD

RUST

SCREW

SHIPS

SPRING

STAINLESS

STRENGTH

STRUCTURE

TOOLS

TUNGSTEN

VANADIUM

WIRES

WOOL

```
T V H E Y O L L A L S J N B
E G D I R B H C P L A T E E
H W O S E L I B O M O T U A
J I C E L S E O H A R D E M
E R W S T R T N P N K L U M
R E E E U E E P L U M I L L
U S R N C T L C D F D S P J
T L C A S I H I Y A K I S M
C C S G A N E C N C T O T I
U Z N N S D A A O T L I A N
R U C A P U V L S U E I I I
T E B M R S Y B A R M M N N
S R M R I T U D L I U B L G
L O O W N R A C K N I V E S
E D A R G Y Q V S G R U S T
S P I H S H T G N E R T S O
```

Solution on Page 288

ACADEMY AWARD

ACTOR

AMERICAN

CALIFORNIA

CHARLES

CHEVALIER

ENVIRONMENTALIST

FILM

GATSBY

IMAGE

JEREMIAH JOHNSON

LOLA

ORDINARY PEOPLE

OSCAR

OUT OF AFRICA

PHILANTHROPIST

POLITICAL

ROLES

SIBYLLE SZAGGARS

STAR

TELEVISION

THE CANDIDATE

THE NATURAL

THE STING

UTAH

WALDO PEPPER

```
S B P J N O I S I V E L E T
R T H E C A N D I D A T E S
A J M R G H A T U C B T S I
G T H E N A T U R A L S E L
G Z A M I O P N E L A I L A
A W C I T O S V I I C P R T
Z A A A S U T C L F I O A N
S L D H E T A M A O T R H E
E D E J H O R L V R I H C M
L O M O T F S I E N L T Y N
L P Y H E A E F H I O N B O
Y E A N L F L P C A P A S R
B P W S O R O T C A U L T I
I P A O L I R E G A M I A V
S E R N A C I R E M A H G N
O R D I N A R Y P E O P L E
```

Solution on Page 288

Answers

Funny Stuff

Aromatherapy

At the Old Ball Game

Plymouth Colony

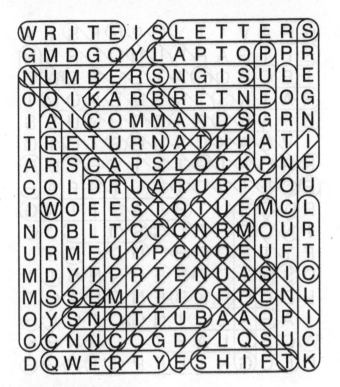

Keyboards

Fitness Club

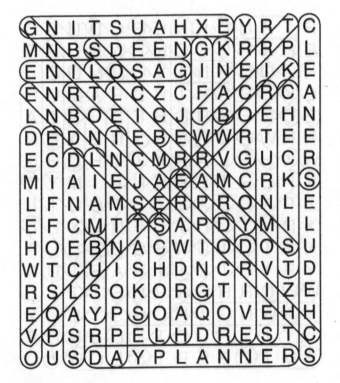

Errands

Really Amazing

City Living

Landslides

Office Supplies

Slow Traffic

Caring for Pets

Indonesia

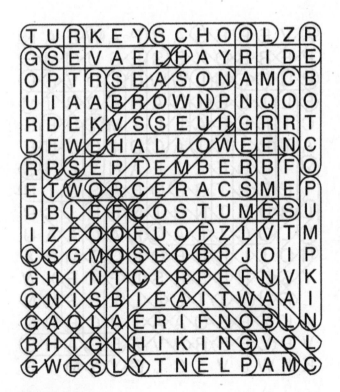

Fall Fun

Flea Market Shopping

Yummy Donuts

Beer

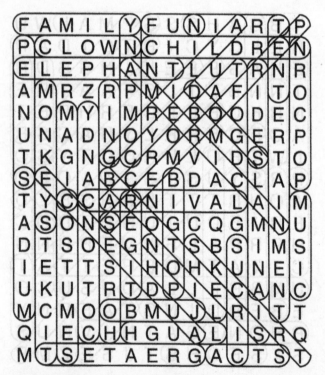

Ringling Brothers

Pet Cats

New Mexico

Nice Times

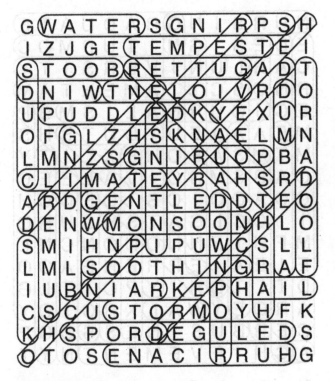

Downpour

Game Night

Open the Door

```
C R R K E A V E X I T G Z T
M O O R Y I G K O S N P U N
A P L C T N G M W R I O Y U
A L E Q O I T A F O W A R T E
S N D W R E R R D O P T U F
M M S E U R A O N O R A H I
C V O M C I G N I D I L S X
B T R O E O E T W R V D S B
O M N H S R R H E M A R F J
N E A U T O M A T I C C M H
K T T J E Z G N T O Y N Q D
C H E G G N I D L I U B H D
O G N S S S A L G T V R E E
L I T K O F M E T A L E C I
H L E S I L L Q Y P O T S C
H Y R E H K C A B K Q G P S
```

Open the Door

Around the Park

```
E G P E I N A W S E G O D Q
H T E C J S L D P H G N K X
U R C W S L I D E A O X L K
T A I O T K N U M P I H C S
G I E V N N L E K B E A C H
P L L K E C H I L D R E N O
D E T D R R E S G N G U B W
D X R G A Z H R I A S D A D
Z A U E P P H V T F Z R L E
G S T E Y C A R O U S E L L
N K A S N L P V R E R G B P
I C R E E K A L I R H G P O
W U B I K E S B I L N O O E
S D E E R V A U V E I J O P
A K O O R B Q S R E W O L F
O C F B Q S N O E G I P N O
```

Around the Park

Carpentry

```
P L A N E R E S B R Q C S I
Y E U S J T R R E T S A M Y
S S C K R G A T V L W S R E
F I N I S H U D E O G T L U
S H M L T O Q T L C E G P L
F C S L R N S C B U N E O G
F O A L E G X E U Q A F R H G
W R O D F S T R O P P U S N
E V O L O U A T P T A S K I
R E T I M P R S E P M A R D
C D N A M Y D N A H A E O L
S A I N L R I O I X O M W O
L R O F I B T C L T C U X M
L T J L A U U D L I U B S K
A O L C E T H A M M E R O E
W O O D L E V E L A T H E X
```

Carpentry

Academic Studies

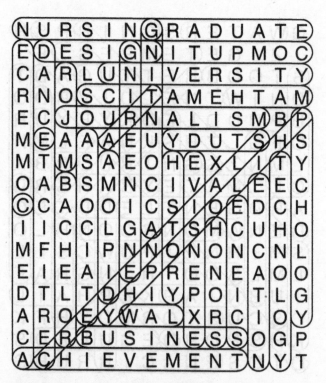

```
N U R S I N G R A D U A T E
E D E S I G N I T U P M O C
C A R L U N I V E R S I T Y
R N O S C I T A M E H T A M
E C J O U R N A L I S M B P
M E A A A E U Y D U T S H S
M T M S A E O H E X L I T Y
O A B S M N C I V A L E C H
C C A O O I C S I O E D C H
I I C C L G A T S H C U O L
M F H I P N O N O N C N O O
E I E A I E P R E N E A T G
D T L T D H I Y P O I T L Y
A R O E Y W A L X R C I O P
C E R B U S I N E S S O G T
A C H I E V E M E N T N Y T
```

Academic Studies

264

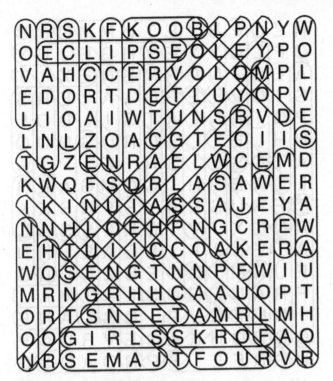

The Twilight Saga

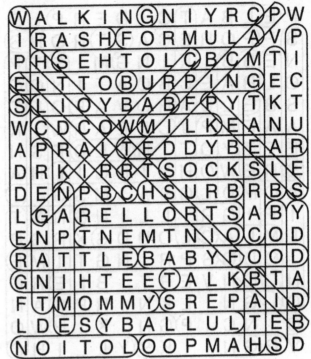

Baby Care

Your Abode

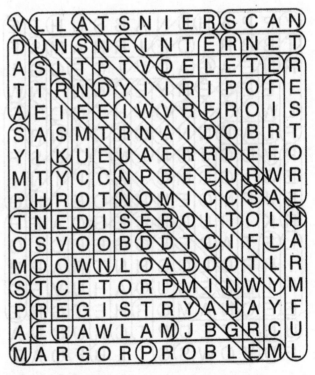

Computer Insecurity

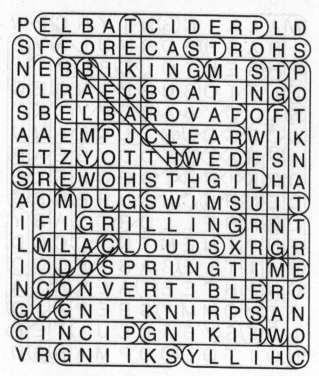

Check the Weather

On the Highway

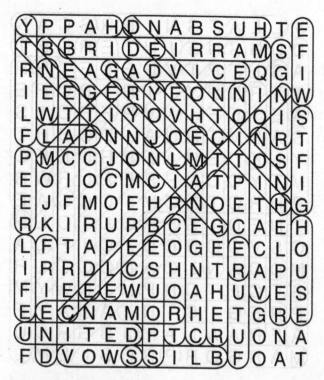

Just Married

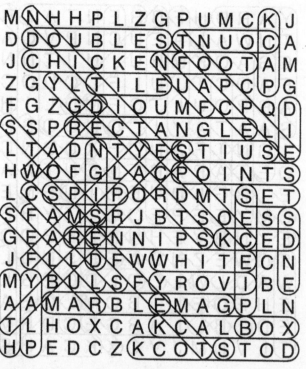

Play Dominoes

Refreshing!

Utility Pole

Win the Lottery

Pillows

Post Office Stop

Fashion Trends

Stovetop

Water Fun

268

Unicycles

On Skates

Sentimental Feelings

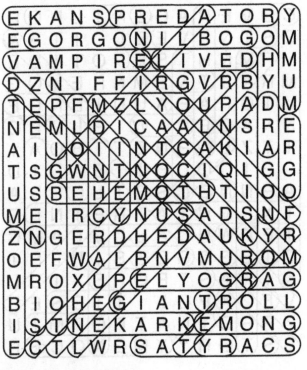

Scary Beasts

Soft Drinks

Short Words

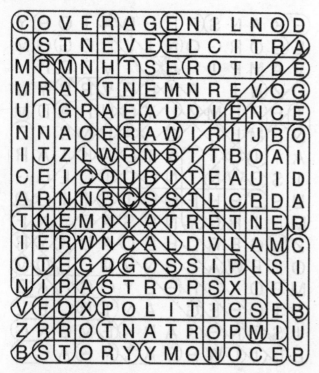

In the News

Vacuum Cleaner

270

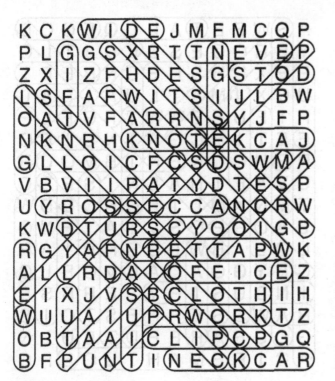

Wear a Tie

Valentine's Day Celebration

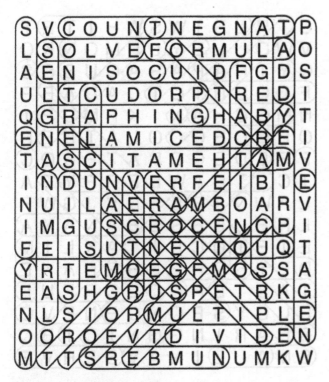

Mathematical

Thanksgiving

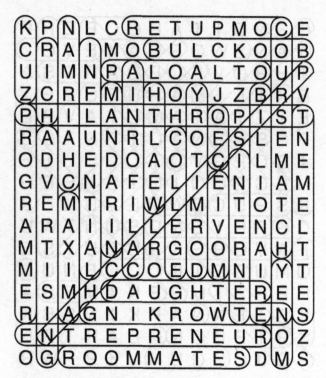

Mark Zuckerberg

Sugarcane

Be Positive!

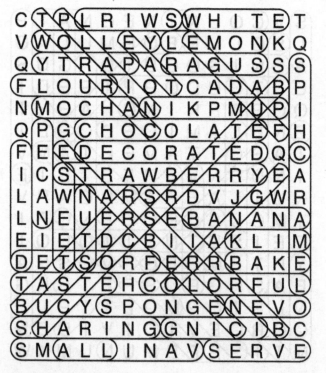

Cupcakes

Creative Drawing

Astrology

Coffee Roast

Bouquet

Walk in the Woods

Tasty Barbecue

Biology Names

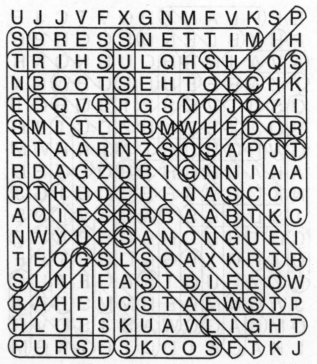

In the Closet

274

Carolina Panthers

Extravagant Gifts

E M N D Y P Y U I N N S A I L
Y O A F A Q L J L F E G A R
S R O F C B J I J A S N W E
D E B R C O T G N I D A O L
B F A R M O A I I E P O R W
J N Y Y Q T R S A K S B K A
E R O H S A E O T A O B E R
T O N K M L P J P L G D R T
T E L I O C A O A W I O S C
Y S P K N G I N C T H C A Y
L D O I R B R U A C A A M A
I S R G H I E A N C R C R K
G P T R V S I A C L B L T F
F L P E P P P H C Q O E R G
N G R I R F J K A H R A U C
Q S M P H N Z F V Q M T D S

Around the Dock

E C G Q D U H G K A B F I T
Q Z U R Y W H Y G I E N E H
E L Y T S Y S H O W E R T T
R R G U G U S U T T B O C H
I E O E S O E P H J O U S K
B V L N W P N G R M D U H D
B A O A S C I S S O R S A N
O H T T X A H L R B C I I O
N S E T R E S P C E B E R L
P S M T T E R C Y I T I S B
E S S U O M A D O O T A A S
R P O L W B H T R M S R W P
M E C Y E L I P M A B R A A
I S X N L N I C L E A N S P
R A U W C O L O R X N F H Q
T Z T I R O N H E A L T H V

Hair Care

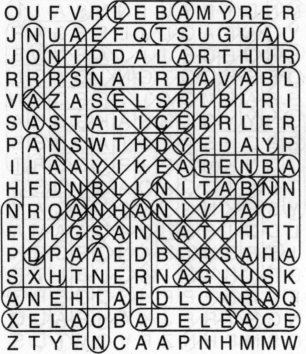

They Start with A

```
O U F V R E B A M Y R E R
J N U A E F Q T S U G U A U
J O N I D D A L A R T H U R
R R R S N A I R D A V A B L
V A Z A S E L S R L B L R I
S A S T A L I C E B R L E R
P A N S W T H D Y E D A Y P
I L A A Y I K E A R E N B A
H L F D N B L N I T A B N I
N R O A N H A N I V L A O I
E E L G S A N L A T L H T T
P D P A A E D B E R S A H A
S X H T N E R N A G L U S K
A N E H T A E D L O N R A Q
X E L A O B A D E L E A C E
Z T Y E N C A A P N H M M W
```

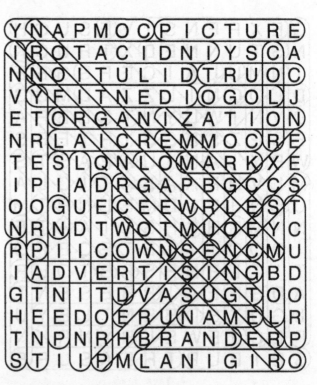

Running

```
R E N E R G Y S F B D F Q R
T E R O U T E C A P A R K A
T E T R I A H S E R F L X J
O Y D A E T S E O H S L G X
R N S F W X A T L J A I N I
T W O L S L E E R E J M Q G
I R C A A H I R R I Q D D F
E I T S U E B A A Q E E G C
Y T S R U I G N R K H R P R A
V E E T C V N S U T X T Z A
Z L N A N R I C A R D I O M
Y H T E A I N E R U T S O P
W T I W S T R E T C H S A D
E A F S U B O P D E R I T B
C P D W A R M U S I C G E F
```

Ready for Bed

```
Z S S R E V O C Q N N Y S I
W O D T N N G D E R I T H W
N O T V H F I T Z L G J O E
N T L E C G E T L H H T W F
M H M L K R I L U F T S E R
O E E D I N E L L O A A R U
O A Q D R P A L L M R N E C
N W Z U K I H L A H L D S Z
A W M C I R F B X U M Q M
P S A Z Q E A T Y H T A W U
X Q X Y X P T D T E S N U S
I K T D R E A D D R H U C I
P Y B F N E N D A T E B R C
C S Z A O L Y T U T E L I B
L Y R O T S S C A D P G S C
H R L E C H K L I M R A W I
```

Trademark Law

```
Y N A P M O C P I C T U R E
I R O T A C I D N I Y S C A
N N O I T U L I D T R U O C
V Y F I T N E D I O G O L J
E T O R G A N I Z A T I O N
N R L A I C R E M M O C R E
T E S L Q N L O M A R K X E
I P I A D R G A P B G C C S
O O G U E C E E W R L E S T
N R N D T W O T M U O E Y C
R P I I C O W N S E N C M U
I A D V E R T I S I N G B D
G T N I T D V A S U G T O O
H E E D O E R U N A M E L R
T N P N R H B R A N D E R P
S T I I P M L A N I G I R O
```

276

On the Menu

Medical Treatment

Dams

Drive a Van

Retirement Life

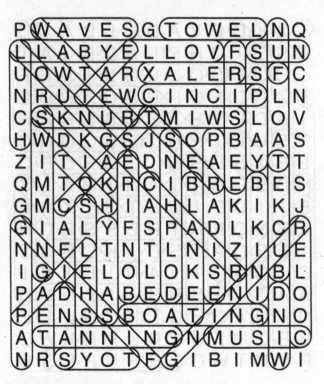

At the Beach

Play a Saxophone

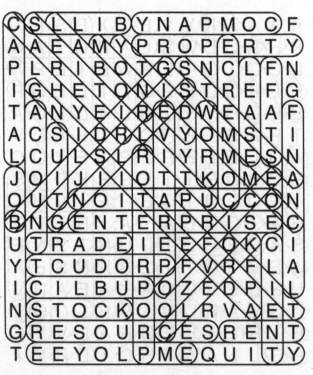

Down to Business

278

Growing Plants

Around the House

Survival Kit

Driving a Porsche

On the Calendar

Cheerleading

Birds

Cute Dachshunds

280

Bernie Sanders

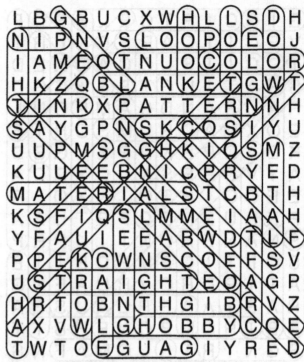

Know Your Knitting

Bake It

Capitalistic

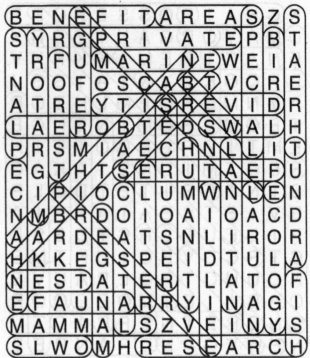

Make Music

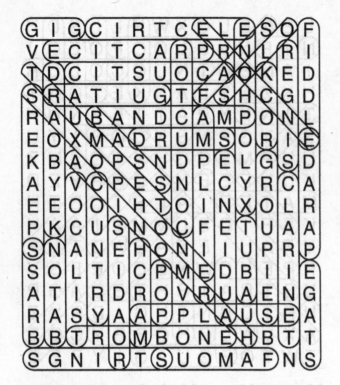

Nature Reserve

Argentina

Things That Shine

Refrigerator Contents

African Wildlife

Play Guitar

Whistle

Night Things

```
C Z P N A B U L C P E E L S
A U L O L D D A R K T E K S
N G A V A A I A I T S R Y U
D I N E R N C G C O O A T N
L E I E L M C O R K W H M R S
E R T O O I S C E L G T A E
S O S O S N E R T N Z H P T
L N N Y T G I T S U N G R E
I S P D A F L T S E R I E K
P E A E R I F P M A C N D N
P I J W E R E W O L F O A A
E V A H S U R B H T O O T L
R O M I D N I G H T B M O B
S M A E R D F V A M P I R E
X H S Y X M O N S T E R S D
S T O R Y V Q U I E T A B E
```

Sports

```
E F I S H C A O C S S Q H Y
K T E N N I S A M N O Y C O
G C G U H Y M A G O C E T L
N Y A N G P R E S W C K A Y
I L M R I A R I O S E C C M
X L V N T C E E H H R O T P
O A G H A A A L F O F H P I
B R O S O S B R S E C X L C
W N Z C B M T S W A R T A S
H I K I N G E Y I C E Y L A
R U G B Y H N R C K W N E A
T L W O B R E P U S M C R O
E M E R T X E R U N N I N G
A W R E S T L E T A R A K O
M S T A D I U M D L E I F L
A Y U V Y Z B U S R F H L F
```

Have a Snack

```
W S L L O R A N G E L P P A
S E V I L O V N R I S I N V
P S E L K C I P A N A N A B
R F I Y D N A C N D S L C F
E A J E R K Y Y O W E V H R
A Y I O N H N Y L T I B O U
D C M S T O R R A C K R S I
S E H L I E C L F S O O E T
J R A I L N O S T P O W G S
U E W E P C S U E O C N D A
H A C J O S N R R P Q I U O
S L C H E E S E N C K E F T
E E C M U S H R O O M S Q R
E G T N A S S I O R C A K E
D A I L Y J V M N N P I D A
S B M S P I C Y T S A T O T
```

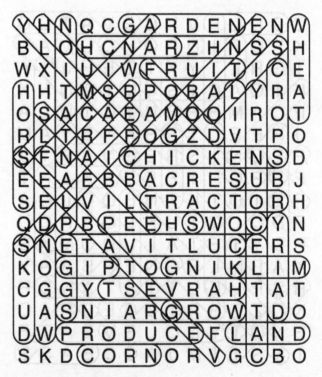

Farm Life

```
Y H N Q C G A R D E N E N W
B L O H C N A R Z H N S S H
W X I U I W F R U I T I C E
H H T M S B P O B A L Y R A
O S A C A E A M O O I R O T
R L T R F P O G Z D V T P O
S F N A I C H I C K E N S D
E E A E B B A C R E S U B J
S E L V I L T R A C T O R H
Q D P B P E E H S W O C Y N
S N E T A V I T L U C E R S
K O G I P T O G N I K L I M
C G G Y T S E V R A H T A T
U A S N I A R G R O W T D O
D W P R O D U C E F L A N D
S K D C O R N O R V G C B O
```

Beads

Look for *S*

Comic Book Convention

Cameras

Mice

Fun Things

The Federal Reserve

Ice Cream for Dessert

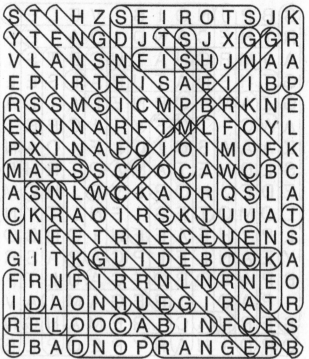

Camping

Throw a Party

Delaware

Coldplay

Strong As Steel

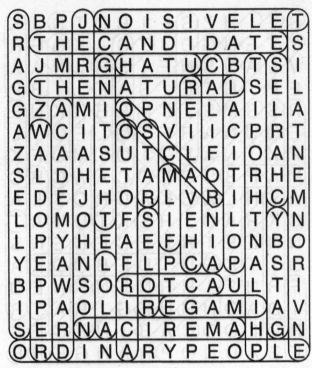

Robert Redford